Evaluating Job-Related Training

A Guide for Training the Trainer

Basil S. Deming
Manager of Human Resource Development
Communications Division
Bendix Aerospace-Electronics

Published by the
American Society for Training and Development
Washington, DC
and
Prentice-Hall, Inc.
Englewood Cliffs, New Jersey

ISBN 013-292292-4

Manufactured in the United States of America.

Published by:
American Society for Training and Development
600 Maryland Avenue, S.W. • Suite 305
Washington, DC 20024

and

Prentice-Hall, Inc.
Englewood Cliffs, New Jersey

For Rose Marie, Elaina, Elisha and Lara,
who sustained me in this labor of love.

Preface

One of the most important things a writer must do is to identify his or her audience. This I have found relatively easy to do. Most readers will be directly involved in training. Either they will be occasional instructors, full-time trainers, training managers or human resource development personnel who are concerned with improving human performance. In fewer cases, the reader will be a manager or analyst whose job it is to evaluate training.

It may appear that I have written this book largely for that last and smallest audience, for I often speak of the trainer or training manager in the third person as I address the "evaluator" directly. In actuality, the book is meant for anyone who is concerned about assessing the quality and effectiveness of training. I have found it most convenient to address the reader as "evaluator" because, regardless of the person's title or organizational asssignment, I am writing to help the reader learn how to actually evaluate training efforts, whether a brief workshop or a massive program.

At the same time, I realize that many, perhaps most, readers will be trainers interested in assessing the quality and effectiveness of their own training efforts. To them I especially dedicate this book, for I am convinced that most productive efforts in the training community come from individuals who are secure enough to question the effectiveness of their own work and who do so regularly.

—Basil S. Deming
November 1982

Table of Contents

Evaluating Job-Related Training

Chapter 1

Introduction

Formal training is one of the most critical enterprises in modern society. Every individual is exposed to formal training, even if this includes only the skill development activities of early schooling—reading, writing, calculating and language usage.

The importance of further formal training is frequently underscored when we express concern over the plight of the "unskilled" worker or of the skilled worker whose skills have become obsolescent in today's rapidly changing technological environment. At the same time, Western industrial societies have become increasingly preoccupied with "productivity," the measure of a person's or organization's ability to turn out quality goods or services in effective and efficient ways. The recent successes of the Japanese have come at some cost to the Western industrial nations and particularly to the United States, which has been hard-pressed of late to maintain parity with Japan in many manufacturing areas, from microcomputers to automobiles. This external threat to our markets exacerbates the problem of doing business competitively and profitably when energy costs and interest rates already peck away at the bottom line.

Private business does not suffer in isolation. Utilities and governments at all levels face similar problems—how to accomplish increasingly complex or large tasks with tighter funding bases and more sophisticated technology. Together, rapid technological change and the need to achieve better productivity constitute a major challenge for modern society. The degree to which we meet the challenge will spell the fate for organizations and individuals alike.

Many tools exist to deal with these dual challenges of changing technology and greater productivity. Among them are the sciences which provide the fundamental thrust toward technological innovation—biology, chemistry, physics and electronics. Engineering tames technology to meet specific manufacturing needs; the social sciences provide ways of managing and understanding this whole complex phenomenon.

However, all of these tools and the innovations we derive through their application eventually must be rendered usable to the work force, whose job it is to actually produce goods and render services. The operator must learn how to operate the sophisticated equipment; the supervisor must learn how to handle people in a way that enourages productive behavior; the analyst must learn how to conceptualize a complex process to understand it as an interacting component of a larger system; and a manager must be able to ask for the right information and make good decisions in the absence of complete data.

The necessary link here is training. If people are not adequately trained to use their knowledge, that knowledge will not flow effectively into the production of goods and services.

This book discusses the evaluation of job-related training. Evaluating training is similar to testing for an electrical conductor's effectiveness. Is the electricity flowing through the conductor? Is there evidence of partial impedence? Can a better conductor be fashioned? Can a less expensive conductor do the job as well? Unlike an electrical conductor, which usually provides consistently high performance as a means for transporting energy to its target, training efforts frequently fail to meet their mark.

The fact that training so often fails is evidence of its complexity. Witness the 1979 nuclear accident at Three-Mile Island. If training were a simple matter, people would get it right the first time. But it is not always simple. It requires talent, trained skills, specialized knowledge and experience. Furthermore, it requires systematic assessment. Feedback is something we always require to improve performance in most any task.

This book covers the major tasks an evaluator must perform when evaluating training, and it defines and illustrates the many evaluation skills required to perform those major tasks. After studying the book, the reader should be able to apply each of these skills in performing the tasks involved in training evaluation. The reader's level of ability will be influenced, of course, by prior experience and training, but the many illustrations and tools provided in the text should assist even the novice in conducting useful training evaluation.

The evaluation tasks and their enabling skills are:

Evaluator Task #1: **Assess the appropriateness and adequacy of instructional objectives (Chapter 2).**

Enabling Skills:
- Ability to classify statements as performance or non-performance.
- Ability to identify performance objectives as dealing with information, intellectual skills, motor skills or attitude.
- Ability to ask appropriate questions regarding the purposes of training.

Evaluator Task #2: **Assess the appropriateness and adequacy of test instruments, test situations and the use of test results for training (Chapter 3).**

Enabling Skills:
- Ability to prescribe performance criteria for instructional objectives.
- Ability to prescribe test items and test situations based upon instructional objectives and performance criteria.
- Ability to prescribe test items and test situations for purposes of diagnosing learner needs, providing feedback on learner performance, certifying the learner as competent and modifying instruction.

Evaluator Task #3: **Assess the appropriateness and adequacy of instructional strategies, both as planned and as carried out in the actual events of instruction (Chapter 4).**

Enabling Skills:
- Ability to apply a comprehensive model of instructional strategy to a given instructional plan.
- Ability to assess the trainer's effectiveness in implementing his instructional strategy.

Evaluator Task #4: **Assess the degree to which learning is transferred from training to actual performance situations (Chapter 5).**

Enabling Skills:
- Ability to match follow-up assessment methods with different types of performance.
- Ability to select or design criteria formats to assist in the assessment process.

Evaluator Task #5: **Assess the endurance of learned performance over time (Chapter 6).**

Enabling Skills:
- Ability to design a time-series study for assessing learner performance over time.
- Ability to recognize situations in which time-series assessment is appropriate.

Evaluator Task #6:   Assess the costs and benefits associated with training (Chapter 7).

Enabling Skills:
- Ability to calculate the cost of training.
- Ability to project the cost of alternatives to training.
- Ability to price the effects of substandard performance.
- Ability to project costs and benefits for non-technical training.
- Ability to project costs and benefits for individual development.

Evaluator Task #7:   Prioritize organizational training efforts in terms of their relative value to the organization (Chapter 8).

Enabling Skills:
- Ability to achieve organizational consensus on the relative value of major training efforts.
- Ability to conduct preliminary assessments of training effectiveness in brief time periods.
- Ability to form recommendations to decision makers regarding the funding and evaluation of training efforts.

Evaluator Task #8: ⸱ Identify training as proactive or reactive (Chapter 9).

Enabling Skills:
- Ability to identify root causes of performance problems.
- Ability to classify causes of performance problems as amenable, not amenable or partially amenable to training solutions.

Chapter 2

What Should They Have Learned?

The training evaluator is advised to begin his or her analysis of training by asking: "What should the trainee have learned as a result of the training?"

The reason for starting with this question is fundamental—no matter what or how much else the trainee learned, if he or she failed to learn the information or develop the skills which are the primary objects of the training, then the training has failed in its central purpose.

If, for example, an air traffic controller has learned the rules and regulations governing commercial air traffic but has not mastered radio interaction procedures with pilots, his or her training has failed to prepare him or her for a fundamental air controller task, one he or she must possess to perform the job adequately. Needless to say, the likelihood of the learner acquiring particular knowledge, skills and attitudes needed for the job is greatly increased when the trainer clarifies for him- or herself, if for no one else, exactly what the learner should be able to do and is inclined to do as a result of instruction.

The simplest way of obtaining answers to the first evaluation question, "What should the trainee have learned as a result of the training?" is to study the trainer's objectives for the learner. This presupposes that the trainer has formulated clear and purposeful objectives.

Many trainers, depending upon their own training and experience, will actually construct either no objectives or objectives which are difficult to comprehend. Where clearly stated objectives for the learner are not yet formulated, the evaluator is in a position to make an important contribution both to the trainer's professional development and to the training under assessment. He or she can do this by helping the trainer articulate the objectives that should be directing the course or program in question.

What follows are two modules geared to transmit the fundamentals of formulating instructional objectives. Self-checks are provided for each module. If you have experience in formulating performance objectives, you may wish simply to read through the modules for ideas on helping trainers in this skill area and to become familiar with terminology used in subsequent portions of the book.

MODULE 1

OBJECTIVE: *To be able to classify statements as performance or non-performance.*

When you have finished this module you will be able to look at a statement about what is to be learned and indicate whether or not it describes, clearly and unambiguously, an observable performance.

RATIONALE: By stating that the learner is able to do something clearly observable to us as a result of instruction, we give ourselves ways of checking or measuring to see if, in fact, learning has occurred. Without clear, observable acts which the learner must perform, we can only guess or infer whether he or she has learned anything.

STANDARD: You will have achieved the ability to distinguish between performance and non-performance statements if you select 80 percent of the statements correctly in the module test.

INSTRUCTION: Consider this statement of an objective: *The community assistance worker will know local sources of help for the elderly, the handicapped and the poor.*
Suppose your job were to design instruction which was geared toward helping the learner to *know* community resources. How would you find out if, at some point during or after your instruction, the learner *knew* the community resources? Is it the kind of *knowing* you can observe directly? If your objective were that the learner know the location of social services, governmental offices and discount stores, you could certainly observe the learner's knowledge, perhaps by asking the learner to describe the location of each place, or by actually watching the learner proceed to the locations.
The problem with a word like "knowing" when setting objectives for learners is that "knowing" cannot be observed directly. You can't really see a person "knowing" his community. You can only infer that he or she knows it more or less, on the basis of how he or she talks about it, who the person interacts with in the community, or how resources are used.
The critical point is that the word "knowing" doesn't usually give us enough information for planning instruction. It doesn't tell us what kinds of skills or knowledge or experiences are most important to the learner.
Now consider this objective:
The community assistance worker will be able to direct clients to those local agencies, social services and businesses which are most appropriate to the client's needs.

Suppose your job were to design instruction geared to helping the learner to achieve this objective—i.e., to actually identify appropriate community offices and businesses for such purposes as obtaining a driver's license, applying for social security or purchasing hardware at a discount. Does this statement give you any more guidance than "*the... worker will know local sources of help for the elderly, for the handicapped and for the poor*"? It certainly narrows the arbitrary number of things you might have the learner do. You can always observe the learner *directing,* whereas you cannot always observe *knowing.*

Consider this objective:

The learner will understand the operation of a printing press.

What could you observe the learner doing that would give you direct evidence that he or she *understands* the operation of a printing press? Is a verbal explanation of how the press functions mechanically a sufficient performance? Or would you insist that the learner be able to actually run the press? How about preventive maintenance? And should he or she be expected to produce a certain quality of print over a number of runs? The verb "understand," like "know," too often fails to supply us with enough information for planning instruction.

Note the greater precision and clarity in the following performance statement:

The learner will demonstrate correct printing press operation procedures by inspecting the press for operational readiness, running an acceptable print through the machine and conducting operator level maintenance of the machine.

Now, consider the following statement:

The manager will come to appreciate the need for delegation of authority.

This is unquestionably a worthy goal. But does it indicate what the manager will be required to do in order to show whether any learning has taken place? Should the manager be required to identify specific areas in which he or she could delegate authority? Or is it sufficient that he or she be able to explain the advantages of delegation?

An appropriate performance statement might be the following:

The manager will be able to formulate a plan for delegating authority to his or her own subordinates.

This performance objective does not necessarily fulfill the need to develop "appreciation" on the manager's part for delegation of authority. It may be but one instructional objective among many which support the trainer's ultimate goal of increasing the likelihood that the manager will choose to delegate. Another useful performance objective might be for the manager to *identify responsibilities which he or she believes would assist in his or her professional development and result in more effective organizational management.*

Self Check

Here are six statements of objectives for learners. Which statements are performance statements, i.e., which ones call clearly and unambiguously for the learner to do something which can be directly observed by the instructor. Circle the performance statements.

1. Know how to operate a lathe.

2. Classify claims into functional categories.

3. Understand the federal budgetary process.

4. Formulate an effective solution to a labor relations problem.

5. Describe the mechanical differences between manual and power brakes.

6. Appreciate the importance of equal opportunity employment.

Did you circle numbers 2, 4 and 5 only? Those are the ones which require acts that can be observed directly. **If you answered correctly for each one, you are ready to take the Module 1 test. Please proceed directly to it.**

If you missed any of the answers above, let's look at each item in turn. At first, objective number 1—know how to operate a lathe—may seem sufficiently observable to qualify as a performance objective. The problem is that ability to operate a lathe is really a matter of degree. The learner may know how to turn on the power, how to mount stock and how to activate the cutting tool, but he or she may lack the skill for producing precision work. The problem with objective number 1 is that it doesn't require or suggest a specific act or acts which can be observed to assess performance, such as producing finished work consistently within acceptable tolerances.

Objective number 2 requires the learner to perform some sort of selecting and categorizing procedure. That procedure can be directly observed and thereby qualifies as a performance statement.

Objective number 3 fails to indicate what the learner must do to show learning. Shall he or she describe the various Congressional committees which appropriate funds or set spending ceilings? Shall the learner explain how political philosophies and partisan interests affect the budget process? Or is it enough that he or she be able to trace a hypothetical budget item from a Congressional committee to full joint Congressional approval? Objective number 3 is too ambiguous to quality as a performance statement.

Objective number 4, however, calls for a specific operation. The learner must actually produce a plan to resolve a problem. Whether that plan must meet certain specific criteria, whether it needs to be fully articulated or simply outlined is yet to be determined. A plan can be observed directly as long as it is recorded in some fashion or even verbalized.

Objective number 5 requires the learner to produce something—in this case a description which should reveal the degree to which he or she comprehends the essential differences between manual and power brakes. Therefore, objective number 5 qualifies as a performance statement.

Objective number 6 fails to specify an observable act and thus does not qualify as a performance statement.

Now try the Module 1 test. You may wish to review the module instruction before you take it. Remember, the suggested standard for your performance is 80 percent accuracy.

MODULE 1 TEST

Circle only the performance statements.

1. Understand how a combustion engine works.

2. Know the difference between legitimate and illegitimate claims for unemployment compensation.

3. Identify pieces which fail to meet specifications.

4. Describe the procedure for inspecting a grain elevator.

5. Appreciate the need for protection in working with radioactive materials.

6. Demonstrate cardiopulmonary resuscitation.

7. Learn the methods for transferring bank funds.

8. See the value in diversified investment.

9. List the five most common causes of highway fatalities.

10. Formulate a plan for evacuating the community in an emergency.

11. Discover a relationship between labor-management communications and organizational productivity.

12. Understand conversational French.

13. Appreciate the versatility of aluminum.

14. Explain the procedure for extruding steel.

15. Assemble a survival kit for wilderness hiking which weighs less than 10 pounds.

You may check your accuracy by reviewing the answers given at the end of this chapter. If you scored 80 percent or better, you are ready for Module 2. If you scored less than 80 percent, you may wish to review Module 1 again.

MODULE 2

OBJECTIVE: To be able to identify performance objectives as dealing with intellectual skills, motor skills, information or attitudes.

When you have finished this module you will be able to identify and classify several given performance objectives into four basic types of human capability.

RATIONALE: Different kinds of human capabilities require different conditions for learning. Learning how to solve math equations may involve the learning principles of repetition and reinforcement and may depend heavily upon several prerequisite math skills. By way of contrast, forming an attitude might involve the principle of human modeling and might rely very little on specific prerequisite skills.

An early step toward planning for instruction then must involve an ability to identify what type of learning is projected for the learner. Once able to identify the type of learning, the instructor can systematically plan instruction which is efficient and effective in terms of learner achievement.

The training evaluator must also be able to identify the type of learning required of the learner or at least be able to assist the trainer in that identification process. Moreover, the evaluator must be as sophisticated in his or her knowledge of human learning capabilities and conditions for learning as the instructional developer. Otherwise, there is little likelihood that the evaluator will have much of a substance to say regarding the appropriateness of objectives and instructional strategies developed for a particular lesson, course or program. This module deals with those human learning capabilities as reflected in performance objectives.

STANDARD: 80 percent accuracy.

INSTRUCTION: To help you learn to identify the four types of human learning capabilities, we will rely upon example as well as partial definition.

> **MOTOR SKILL.** A motor skill is a physical skill. While many motor skills involve learned thought patterns, they are easily distinguished from intellectual skills. Some obvious examples of motor skills are jumping rope, tying shoe laces or running. Most motor skill objectives for juvenile, adolescent and adult learners are complex enough to contain several component skills, e.g., swimming the length of the pool, a requirement for graduation in many school systems. Swimming embraces subskills involving leg kick, stroke, head movement, and several other component skills.
>
> In addition to learning which is almost exclusively physical in nature, motor skills are often acquired along with intellectual skills and knowledge in performing complex activities such as driving, preparing meals, playing tennis and carpentry.

INTELLECTUAL SKILL. An intellectual skill is a thinking skill. Just as many motor skills involve thought patterns, so too many intellectual skills involve motor activity. But it is the mental activity which is being emphasized. Reading a text is an example of this. Visual acuity and visual tracking skills (motor) are involved in reading, but the ability to identify written letters and words as meaningful symbols of concrete and abstract entites is an intellectual skill. Categorizing objects into classes and applying rules to solve problems are also intellectual skills.

INFORMATION. Information can be an isolated fact, a statement of opinion, a piece of propaganda, an organized body of knowledge. It can be accurate or distorted, understood or misunderstood. It can be conveyed through various media and forms. It can provide the knowledge necessary for learning the names of things, for classifying things into categories, for learning rules and for solving problems; even for creating new problems to be solved.

Of critical importance, however, is that information and intellectual skills learning are not the same. Knowing—having information available for memory retrieval—is necessary for an intellectual act, but it does not require the same conditions for learning. For example, should an Internal Revenue Service trainee not understand the precise meanings conveyed by the terms "single taxpayer" and "corporate taxpayer," we could give him or her definitions and examples of those terms or concepts in order to understand the concepts accurately. His or her attainment of those concepts would be an instance of what Gagne has labeled concept-formation, a type of intellectual skill.

Now let us assume the trainee has formed these two concepts for him- or herself. At some later point during instruction, he or she learns that corporate accounts are handled differently than single tax accounts. This is a statement of fact, a segment of information which the trainee is now expected to retain in his or her memory. He or she has not learned a new concept in this instance, but a fact. At a still later point during instruction, he or she may draw upon that bit of information along with other pieces of information to perform an intellectual skill, e.g., classifying accounts into categories of profit and nonprofit corporations.

In brief, information, in addition to whatever value it may hold simply as information, serves as building blocks for intellectual operations. This distinction between information and intellectual skill is a crucial one for purposes of developing instruction and assessing learner performance.

ATTITUDE. There are several definitions of attitude, each reflecting the bias of one or another school of psychology. Many believe attitudes to be purely internal states. Others believe them to be tendencies to act in response to external stimuli. In either case, most will agree that attitude involves personal beliefs, assumptions, perceptions, misperceptions, information, feelings or preferences in relation to a given object, person, institution, statement or event.

For purposes of designing instruction, it is helpful at least to accept the observable choices of certain behaviors as direct indicators of attitude, e.g., choosing consistently to wear safety goggles and gloves while spot welding, or choosing to assist another worker having difficulty on the shop floor. These choices may evidence that the learner in the first case appreciates the danger inherent in not wearing goggles and gloves and in the second instance believes that mutual assistance on the shop floor is better than everyone looking out only for themselves.

Self Check

Here are eight objectives for learners. Mark each one according to whether it represents a *motor skill* (MS), an *intellectual skill* (IS), *information* (I) or an *attitude* (A).

_____ 1. States the procedure for handling cars parked illegally in no parking zones.

_____ 2. Chooses to ask employees for ideas to improve quality of work life.

_____ 3. Distinguishes between operational and nonoperational pipelines.

_____ 4. Draws a straight line.

_____ 5. Recites the code of conduct.

_____ 6. Chooses to extinguish all lights when leaving work area.

_____ 7. Scores at or above the marksman level.

_____ 8. Formulates a plan to reroute traffic.

The answers are shown at the bottom of the page. If you answered each one correctly, take the Module 2 test.

If you missed any of the answers, reconsider them briefly. Notice the key verbs in numbers 1 and 5. They signal that you have an objective dealing with information. You want the learner to be able to call upon a segment or a whole body of information, formulas, functions, definitions, dates, names, events, etc., which he or she has learned previously.

Now look again at numbers 3 and 8. In these objectives, the learners are asked to perform mental or intellectual skills— distinguishing between two conditions and formulating a plan. Their successful accomplishment relies partially upon knowledge, i.e.,

1. I, 2. A, 3. IS, 4. MS, 5. I, 6. A, 7. MS, 8. IS

what characterizes a pipeline as operational or nonoperational; what principles need to be considered in rerouting traffic. But actually performing these tasks is not synonymous with knowledge. Rather, they are intellectual acts which use knowledge.

Consider numbers 4 and 7. They may also presuppose knowledge, i.e., that learners know a straight line when they see one; that they know the proper technique for firing a weapon. However, the performances called for in 4 and 7 are basically concerned with physical coordination involving muscle movement and control.

Numbers 2 and 6 begin with the word "chooses." It signals choice or preference, and it is from that choice or preference that we directly infer attitude.

Now try the Module 2 test. The acceptable level of accuracy is 80 percent.

MODULE 2 TEST

Label each objective below an intellectual skill (IS), a motor skill (MS), information (I) or an attitude (A).

_____ 1.   Types at least 30 words per minute, copying from a text.

_____ 2.   Identifies wiring mockups as sound or faulty.

_____ 3.   Demonstrates proper use of a hand plane by shaving smooth a wood surface.

_____ 4.   Describes the procedure for inspecting meat.

_____ 5.   Chooses to proofread all typing before turning it over to the supervisor.

_____ 6.   Creates a blueprint for an industrial sprinkler system.

_____ 7.   Explains the function of a pulley.

_____ 8.   Voluntarily places tools in their proper storage places after finishing work.

_____ 9.   Designs an emergency plan for evacuating an urban area.

_____ 10. States the procedure for validating identification of building visitors.

_____ 11. Demonstrates cardio-pulmonary resuscitation.

_____ 12. Diagnoses an engine malfunction.

_____ 13. Chooses to inspect brake linings carefully for cracks, loose fittings and excessive wear.

_____ 14. Writes the formulas for computing area and volume.

_____ 15. Describes how to register to vote.

_____ 16. Demonstrates the procedure for transferring a neck-injured patient from one flat surface to another.

_____ 17. Calculates claims benefits in accordance with appropriate manuals.

_____ 18. Volunteers to practice as necessary outside of regular training sessions.

_____ 19. Spot welds within tolerances and time limits.

_____ 20. Translates computer programs from one systems language to another.

When you have finished, check your accuracy against the answers provided at the end of this chapter. If you scored 80 percent or better you are ready to move on. If you scored less than 80 percent, you may wish to review the module again.

Assessing the Appropriateness and Adequacy of Instructional Objectives

At this point, you are able to determine whether the trainer has identified, in a clear, observable manner, what the learner should be able to do as a result of instruction. Moreover, you are able to identify performance objectives by the basic types of human learning they represent—intellectual skills, motor skills, information or attitudes.

These evaluation skills have an instrumental value in that they prepare the evaluator to approach his or her first major evaluation task. That task is *to determine whether a course's or program's instructional objectives fully and accurately convey the primary purposes of training.*

Applying the Skills

Just the ability to write clear, observable statements about learning requires specialized training. Therefore, the evaluator needs to understand that the trainer faces a considerable professional challenge as he or she attempts to formulate performance objectives which not only are written clearly but which convey fully and accurately the primary purposes of training. To be comprehensive, the objectives should include all the types of human learning that require attention, e.g., changes in attitude and information acquisition, or the development of motor skills and intellectual skills.

In order to assess the appropriateness and adequacy of a trainer's instructional objectives, an evaluator must be able to ask critical questions about the primary prupuses of training. If the trainer cannot answer these questions, it is a good sign that he or she has not understood the purposes sufficiently to have developed a training course or program that fully meets the needs of the learner or the organization.

A set of questions and guidelines is provided below as a reference point for working with the trainer. But before turning to these questions, let's briefly consider some examples of instructional objectives and their potential for improvement through an evaluator's intervention.

Let's begin by examining a brief set of objectives formulated for a nuclear power plant course given to technicians whose job it is to monitor instruments and take preventive or corrective action when necessary within the control room of the power plant.

Objectives

1. Explain the function of each warning system and monitoring mechanism.

2. List the warning signals and state their meaning.

3. Describe the sequence of steps prescribed for each system warning signal.

4. List all rules regarding control room security and safety.

Let's presume that we as evaluators are not intimately familiar with the subject matter in question. This lack of knowledge requires that we ask questions which will yield critical information and will prompt the trainer to reflect critically upon his or her objectives. Ultimately, the trainer may have to obtain assistance from knowledgeable personnel in order to answer many of these questions.

In the case of power plant technical training, we may ask whether the trainee is given an opportunity to experience firsthand the warning signals which would appear in the actual control room. Here we are concerned with the technician's ability to transfer learning from the training setting to the job. (This subject is treated in depth in Chapter 5.) Two appropriate objectives which represent this concern are the following:

1. Detect warning signals in a real or simulated control room under simulated emergency conditions.

2. Take immediate and appropriate action upon detecting each warning signal.

These two objectives assure that attempts will be made to develop training in a way that bridges the critical gap between learning information and intellectual skill development. The former involves the simple acquisition of facts whereas the latter involves the formation of new thinking skills.

In the case of the nuclear power plant technician, he or she may learn several sets of information, e.g., a red light on Panel A indicates a voltage overload or a pressure gauge reading above 10,000 PSI is a signal for releasing a corresponding pressure valve. However, thinking skills come into play when the technician must detect these signals within the total environment of the control room. In this case he or she must learn to recognize an entire battery of signals in context. Each signal comes from a particular location and represents a particular systems function. The technician must not only recognize a light, a sound or a gauge reading, but must be able to relate that signal to the system function it represents in order to take appropriate action. Moreover, if more than one signal is activated, the technician must be able to react to a situation in which a complex combination of problems occurs simultaneously.

Giving the learner opportunities to apply what he or she has learned is a fundamental training principle. Unfortunately, it is perhaps the most neglected of all training tenets. Trainers typically put a great deal of effort into organizing a body of information to present to the learner but much less into constructing opportunities for application of knowledge in a real or highly simulated job environment.

This common failure to provide the learner with opportunities to apply learning is understandable in the light of conventional training practice in which training occurs totally within the confines of a traditional classroom. It may take an evaluator armed with a few critical questions to free the trainer from the conventional classroom mentality. It then becomes a challenge for the organization to provide whatever support is necessary for the trainer to design applied settings for successful transfer of learning.

Let's consider another set of objectives, this time for training given to physicians and medical technicians who handle radioactive isotopes in performing their medical research.

Objectives

1. Identify the radioactive isotopes currently in common usage at the Institute.

2. Describe the safety procedures recommended for using each isotope.

3. List the administrative steps required by the Institute before radioactive isotopes may be used.

4. Identify cleaning procedures appropriate for neutralizing radioactive spills.

5. Describe the procedure to be following in securing a lab area after a radioactive spill.

6. Identify RAD levels with potential effects on human tissue and organs.

Again we work from the position of an evaluator who is not a subject matter specialist. Therefore, we again begin by questioning the primary purposes of training. As we probe, we find that the Institute's chief concern is over lax safety practices regarding the use of radioactive isotopes. We learn that the main problem is not so much lack of knowledge regarding proper procedures or of potential consequences, but rather habitual avoidance of many procedures due to the inconvenience and delay they cause the researcher or technician in initiating and completing his or her work.

This realization should prompt us as evaluators to question whether the training, as reflected in its objectives, is designed to deal effectively with the problem of lax safety habits. There is no pat solution to this problem, but a few suggestions may be worth trying. Consider the addition of the following objectives:

Objectives

1. Simulate the safety procedures required for the six most commonly used isotopes.

2. Demonstrate the cleaning procedures recommended for using these six isotopes.

3. Choose to perform each step in each safety procedure; perform each cleaning procedure carefully and thoroughly.

The addition of these objectives is predicated on two basic principles of human behavior. The first is that we tend to perform tasks which have become habitual or routine more readily than tasks to which we are unaccustomed, especially if those tasks are fundamentally unpleasant or neutral in character. Thus, the person who prepares supper on most evenings of the week generally takes its preparation in stride, whereas the person who cooks infrequently may have to work up his or her courage before starting to prepare a meal. Trainers often fail to apply this principle to their training, much to the disservice of the learner.

A second principle of behavior is very similar—performing a physical task is more conducive to learning it than merely observing it. Performing a sequence of acts, e.g., applying cleaner, wiping it uniformly over a contaminated or simulated contaminated area, properly disposing of the applicator, marking the area for ready identification, etc., are tactile activities. It stands to reason that the learner will more readily master the task and make it part of his or her behavioral response pattern if his or her response is triggered by tactile memory stimulation as well as perceptual.

In our present case, the trainer should consider giving the physicians and technicians ample opportunity and direction in performing these relatively simple but literally life-saving safety procedures in the radioactive isotope lab. This may mean overcoming any embarrassment over making high-paid professionals perform menial labor. If it increases the likelihood that they will use the procedures in the unsupervised environment of their own labs, it should be strongly considered.

Asking the Important Questions

In addressing the questions asked about the objectives described above, we relied upon a knowledge of learning principles. Indeed, a training evaluator's ability to function effectively depends in part upon a knowledge of learning principles. Yet, perhaps a more crucial prerequisite for the evaluator is the ability to ask probing questions and provide direction for the trainer in his or her own analysis of the course or program.

What follows is a set of questions addressing the four major types of human learning; they may be usefully posed during a review of instructional objectives. Each question is followed by a discussion of its role in the analysis process so that the evaluator may understand the purpose and value of the question and may follow it up with other pertinent questions and suggestions as he or she sees fit.

Information

1. Is the information to be learned clearly defined?
This can be ascertained most readily by analyzing the instructional objectives to see if they meet some reasonable criteria:
  a. Is the performance clearly identified? In other words, is there any doubt about what the learner should be able to do as a result of instruction?
  b. Can the performance be observed or measured? Here we look for some direct way of telling whether the learner can really do what the trainer intends. Moreover, if performance can be measured against some reasonable standard, the trainer can assess degrees of learning.
  c. Do the objectives comprise a coherent whole? In studying instructional objectives, the evaluator should expect to find that they present a complete picture of what the training is about. If they do not, it signals that the trainer was not able to fully grasp how each major purpose of the training fits together to serve the learner and the organization.

2. Is the information based on a current training needs analysis or occupational analysis?

It is common for instructional planners to include information that once served a purpose but no longer assists the learner in performing the job. The United States Armed Services, noted for their heavy investment and considerable experience in developing training programs, have saved several millions of dollars over the past decade by systematically assessing the job-relatedness of their training programs and eliminating or altering instructional programs, courses or segments of courses that no longer meet current job needs. Therefore, it should not be surprising if, over time, the original course information you review has also become obsolete. If there has been no attempt to validate the training objectives in an appropriate period of time, the evaluator may wish to recommend that an occupational survey or a training needs analysis be conducted. There is no universal rule of thumb for determining how long training remains valid. It depends upon how rapidly the conditions or methods of job performance change. In a high technology environment, entry-level training may need revision every time it is presented. In a craft which has undergone little change over the years, no validation may ever be necessary on the assumption that since the instructor learned the craft, little has changed which would affect the training.

Most trainers are reasonably competent in the business of organizing instructional information and presenting it to the learner. However, many trainers have not had experience in training needs analysis and certainly very few will have any knowledge of occupational analysis.

Training needs analysis involves studying job performance to determine what information, skills or attitudes are necessary for job performance beyond those the learner already brings to the organization (such as reading or computational skills). Occupational analysis is a study of what job functions and tasks are common to an entire occupation or a subset of an occupation through the use of interviews and surveys. Where the trainer is not conversant with these training validation methods, the evaluator may wish to refer him or her to an appropriate source (see references at end of chapter).

3. Is it necessary for the learner to memorize the details of information called for in the job or is it sufficient to be able to readily access information as it is necessary? And what does the learner do with this information?

People tend to do things they know how to do well. It is perhaps for this reason that trainers tend to plan their instruction largely around information acquisition. However, the requirements of a job may call for far less information acquisition than is reflected in the training but far more skill development.

An example will demonstrate this condition. There are more than 20 different types of railroad car hand brakes presently in use on one of the major railroad lines in this country. It might be tempting for a trainer to require that the learner be able to recall something about all 20 types. However, it would be far more effective and efficient for that trainer to design into the training program sufficient hands-on experience with the most common types so that the learner enters the job already able to handle the few types which comprise the large majority of the hand brakes he or she will encounter rather than knowing what makes each hand brake distinct, including several he or she may not encounter for months.

A test the evaluator should bring to the information objectives given for any training is whether the information will assist the learner in some discernible way to perform or whether it will support the development of appropriate attitudes. If the information conveyed by an objective cannot meet this criteria, it should be considered a candidate for removal or modification.

4. Is some information more crucial than other information?

A common complaint of trainers and school teachers is that they have too little time to cover the curriculum. Because they will always have to work within practical time constraints, trainers should prioritize their objectives for the learner. As the example of many types of hand brakes suggests, some things are more likely to be encountered on the job than others. Moreover, some tasks are more important than others, regardless of frequency. Thus, information bearing on the physical apprehension of suspects may be far more important in police officer training than information regarding the routine filing of reports.

The failure to prioritize can mean that the trainer tries to cover too much in the allotted time. In so doing, he or she lessens the likelihood of the learner mastering the crucial knowledge since the learner is forced to spread thin his or her time and energy in trying to absorb all the information. Better the learner master the important things and learn the rest on the job than go to the job partially prepared on every dimension of work but insufficiently prepared on the most crucial dimensions.

Intellectual Skill

1. Is the learner required to learn new concepts or procedures?

A clear sign that the major purposes of training have not been adequately represented is an absence of intellectual skill objectives. After all, the purpose of most training is that people be able to perform tasks they could not perform before or perform them better than they were able to before. Moreover, performing tasks typically involves either learned motor skills or learned intellectual skills and often some combination of both.

Learned information is usually instrumental, i.e., it is necessary in assisting the learner to perform but it is not the ability to perform itself. Thus the railroad brakeman may need to know that all manual hand brakes call for one basic method of setting and releasing, while power hand brakes call for another. However, he or she also needs to develop the ability to identify each basic type of brake when encountered (intellectual skill) and the ability to set and release those brakes safely and effectively (motor skill).

To analyze the objectives for appropriate inclusion of intellectual skills, we can ask about *concepts* and *procedures* since they form the substance for most intellectual skills.

A tax examiner needs to be able to identify a number of different tax forms (concepts) in order to code, edit and process (procedures) each form appropriately. He or she also needs to understand a variety of alpha/numeric symbols and codes (concepts). For each form and each symbol and code, an operational concept must be formed. For example, he or she must identify Forms 1040A, 1040NB, 1040B&F and 1040X, each with their appropriate sets of procedures. He or she must also be able to identify each alpha/numeric symbol with the operation it performs.

Concepts are the building blocks for rules, principles or procedures, which in turn are the major components of job tasks. When a tax examiner processes a return, he or she applies the appropriate symbols and codes in a specific set of procedures, such as those shown here in a performance objective.

> *Code, edit and process Forms 1040A, 1040NB, 1040B&F and 1040X returns by means of initial entries and edits.*

If all instructional objectives for the tax examiner trainee were information objectives, such as being able to describe the differences between various forms or being able to list the steps in the code and edit process, the evaluator would know—by studying the basic purposes of the training—that the objectives were inadequate representations of those purposes.

2. What are the standards for learner performance?

It is one thing to state that the tax examiner trainee, upon completing his or her training, should be able to code, edit and process forms. It is another to prescribe a standard for performance which the graduate must attain. Are two errors per form within an acceptable range of performance? Are 10 errors? And what about speed? Is it sufficient that the graduate complete one case a day, or one an hour or more?

It is for entry-level training that these questions are particularly appropriate. A great deal of calculation may go into deciding just how much training is appropriate before the trainee graduates to the job. But basically the decision hinges on two questions:

1. Is there a performance baseline below which job performance is decidedly unacceptable?

2. Beyond what performance level is it cost-ineffective or organizationally counterproductive to train the learner?

These questions will be addressed in detail in Chapter 7.

Should no performance standards be evident in the training objectives, the evaluator should at least establish whether the trainer has an implicit standard for assessing the performance of the learner. In many organizations, no one fails entry-level training. This fact does not reflect a humanitarian desire to see everyone succeed. It reflects instead an organization's inability or unwillingness to set precise standards and hold trainees to them. It does not have to be this way. Air traffic control candidates, among others in the federal sector, must meet clear and reasonably rigorous performance standards in order to pass their entry-level training.

Standards need not be perceived as barriers to reasonably qualified trainees. Standards tend to benefit both the job candidate and the organization because they evoke responsible behavior. The learner realizes he or she is responsible for achieving a stipulated level of competency, and the organization, largely through the offices of the trainer, realizes its responsibility for providing learning activities which enable willing candidates to succeed.

A caveat is in order at this point. Not all training lends itself to precise standards. An evaluator may find, for example, that a course on interpersonal communications skill development defies any arbitrary set of performance standards. This may be true of many types of training in which skill development is open-ended, i.e., in which participants may come to the training in various stages of readiness and the range of learning between individuals may be enormous. Standards should be used where they are useful and avoided where they are arbitrary or inhibiting.

3. Will the job require the learner to use particular reference or research skills?

Many desk jobs require that a rather substantial body of knowledge be brought to bear on specific actions or cases. A tendency the evaluator should watch for is an instructional emphasis on the knowledge itself to the neglect of the skills needed for referencing the appropriate sources of knowledge.

The laws and procedures governing Social Security claims are so numerous and complex that they fill several volumes of text. Many experienced claims process personnel learn a large portion of this information over a long period of time. But in many claims cases— even for the experienced claims worker—access to the reference manuals (or computer tapes) is essential. The ability to use references is necessary for successful job performance, and therefore it should be treated adequately in the training. In turn, the instruction given to reference skill development should be clearly reflected in the instructional objectives. Many jobs exist in both the public and private sector that require reference or research skills. The evaluator should be certain those skills are addressed in the training for those jobs.

4. Must human interaction skills be developed as partial preparation for the job?

Delivery of human services continues to grow in our post-industrial society. This means that more and more people deal directly with clients as an integral part of their jobs. The trainer must understand the nature of each encounter the learner will regularly undergo in the course of performing his or her job, and that understanding should be reflected in the training objectives. If it is important that an interviewer ask probing questions to elicit information of a sensitive nature, e.g., a client's emotional state or financial status, then the skills required for that task should be articulated lest they be ignored in the preparation of actual instruction.

Motor Skill

1. Is the learner required to learn any physical tasks?

In an earlier section of this chapter, physical skill activities were characterized as typically accompanying intellectual skill activities. One simple example of this is the operation of a lathe. Depending upon the composition of the operator's tasks, it might be predominantly intellectual or physical.

In one plant where most labor is still manual and heavily supervised, a lathe operator might find his or her tasks composed primarily of retrieving and mounting stock, activating the cutting tool, applying appropriate pressure on the cutting bar, visually inspecting the cut for completion and removing and stacking the stock. These are tasks which primarily require motor skills—retrieving, mounting, activating, removing and stacking.

In another plant where work has been partially automated, a lathe operator may not need to retrieve and mount stock or even perform the cutting operation. Those functions may be carried out through automation. However, as in many Japanese plants, the operator may be required to inspect the lathe periodically for adjustment of tool position, for proper cooling, and for elementary maintenance needs. He or she may also be encouraged to generate ideas for improving the work process itself. In this latter plant, the lathe operator's tasks are as much intellectual as physical.

Suffice it to say here that the evaluator should review instructional objectives to ascertain that physical skills needed to perform job tasks, whether they be primary or secondary to intellectual skills, are adequately represented.

2. Do the motor skills require a specific mastery level, e.g., accuracy, speed or consistency?

This is much the same question as posed under Intellectual Skill, i.e., what are the standards for training performance? Again, one must know (a) whether there is a level of performance below which an individual's performance is deemed unacceptable; and (b) whether it is cost-effective or consistent with organizational goals to train beyond a certain level of performance.

3. Are there safety procedures or precautions to be learned?

Depending upon the nature of the job, physical safety may be an extremely important dimension of job performance. In many cases, failure to observe and apply safety precautions meticulously can result in severe injury or death.

Whenever safety is a factor in job performance, the evaluator should make sure that it is accounted for in terms of motor skill acquisition. This point is easily overlooked but crucial. It is normally not sufficient to relegate safety to information learning. Safe job performance is a matter of acquired habit, and habits are formed through practice and application—not through simple exposure to information.

Safety can be built into the instructional objectives as a dimension of performance standards. For example, in dismounting a moving railroad car, a brakeman must follow a procedure which has specific safety precautions built in:

a. Do not dismount until the car is moving at 4 MPH or less.
b. Face in the direction of the train movement.
c. Look for proper clearance of physical obstructions.
d. Place the outside foot firmly on the ground.
e. Follow through with the inside foot as you release the hand rails.

Now it may be that the details of job performance are so numerous that their inclusion as standards in the instructional objectives would swell the objectives to such an extent that no one would bother reading them. The point here is not that the trainer should account somewhere for everything within the structure of the instructional objectives but that he or she should somehow account somewhere for everything of crucial importance. It may be, for example, that standards of performance, to include safety standards, are simply given for each lesson of a training course. Nevertheless, it is sound practice for the evaluator to check for their inclusion somewhere in the training package. Standards should be evident wherever they are appropriate, and they should be consistent with the performance objectives themselves, if not a part of them.

4. Can and should the motor skills be practiced in an actual or simulated situation?

In an earlier portion of this chapter, an example was given of the nuclear power plant technician who had to learn to integrate his or her knowledge of the several power plant systems in such a way that he or she could respond quickly and correctly to indicators of system imbalance or failure. All the knowledge at one's disposal goes for naught if it cannot be applied in some effective manner.

The use of simulation and on-the-job training has taken many imaginative forms, perhaps the most graphic being the zero-gravity simulators used for training astronauts. The use of simulation will be discussed in detail in Chapter 4.

At this point in the evaluator's analysis, he or she simply wants to raise the question in terms of what the learner is expected to be able to do as a result of training. For example, if the power plant technician is expected to perform at mastery level as soon as he or she goes on the job, he or she had better have training experiences which duplicate in faithful detail the contingencies he or she is most apt to face on the job. This is especially true of physical skill learning, where tasks may need to be performed quickly and flawlessly in stressful situations.

Attitude

1. Are there any concerns about the learner's attitude toward the topic of training?

The answer to this question, when put to entry level training, is usually "no," for most people approach new jobs with open minds and enthusiasm. However, there are some topics more appropriate to inservice training which raise emotional issues for many participants.

Consider, for example, Equal Employment Opportunity (EEO) training. Many managers approach this subject with a mixture of fear and anger. They are fearful that they are about to lose their prerogative to hire people they believe are best suited for the jobs and the units for which the managers are responsible, and they are angry that their discretion is questioned. EEO training is often mandatory rather than optional, and so the manager may come to the training in a less than positive frame of mind. To address this delicate matter in the course of actual training delivery requires ingenuity, skill and fortitude on the part of the trainer. The objectives of instruction should therefore reflect, at least indirectly, the intended attitudinal impact the trainer should have upon the learner. These objectives will provide a starting point for the trainer in this difficult area of planning.

Earlier in this chapter, attitudinal objectives were described in performance terms. We used verbs such as "choose" and "volunteer" to exemplify how the trainer could establish observable indicators of attitudinal change. Thus, for example, the trainer might project the following instructional objective:

> *The manager chooses to construct and defend a plan for broadening his job candidate search strategies.*

In terms of instructional activities, the trainer may wish to assign managers in the EEO training session to work in small groups to brainstorm ideas for expanding their usual methods of soliciting job candidates, then ask the managers to construct detailed plans for their own units individually. The key evidence of attitudinal change may come in the care with which the manager constructs his plan and the effort he expends in defending the plan on the basis of sound EEO principles.

The evaluator must realize that the trainer is on soft ground whenever dealing with attitudinal change. It is difficult to devise objectives which provide incontrovertible evidence of attitude change and even more difficult to devise means for observing or measuring those changes. (The trainer can be referred to Robert Mager's handbook on developing attitudinal objectives called *Goal Analysis* [Fearon Press]. Mager's writing is lucid, concise and light, so it offers an excellent introductory study of the topic.) The main purpose of developing instructional objectives which address learner attitude is to prompt effective instructional strategies which in turn may elicit that change in the learner.

2. Are there old habits that need to be extinguished and new habits that require reinforcement?

People's behavior to a large extent is a product of their upbringing. As such, little of that behavior has been seriously examined through self-analysis, and relatively few people have been through psychotherapy. Therefore, it usually comes as a shock to people that their unconscious ways of behaving are objectionable, either on ethical or economic grounds.

So, for example, we may consider the typical behavior of unit supervisors during times of severe organizational cutbacks. These times are pleasant for no one. At best, they are filled with anxiety over the unknown and depression over reduced chances for advancement. At worst, they are accompanied by fear of unemployment and loss of self-esteem. In addition to a pervasive sense of personal loss, productivity may decline dramatically.

So what would one wish of supervisors—not just first-line supervisors, but supervisors at every level of management—in times of organizational stress and reduction? Experts on organizational health suggest that one would want open and ongoing communication with employees—communication that involves listening as well as speaking. Even if all the news is bad news, at least open communications allow employees to know they are not being kept in ignorance to serve some dark purpose of management. It also serves as a means of self-therapy as it allows employees to express their feelings about what is happening to them.

Supervisors typically become supervisors on the basis of things other than their ability to communicate openly with employees. They may be efficient organizers of work, they may possess much expertise in their field, or they may be good at implementing management directives. Whatever the reasons, they often have little to do with human interaction skills.

Imagine then the job a trainer faces in interpersonal communications training for supervisors, particularly during times of organizational stress. To use the terms of behavioral psychology, there are behaviors to be extinguished and behaviors to be reinforced. Out with the old ineffective behaviors and in with more appropriate ones. Thus the trainer may project the following performance objective:

> *The learner will choose to employ techniques of open communication when involved in stressful personal interactions.*

To enable the learner to meet this objective, the trainer may have to devise all sorts of instructional strategies—modeling, role-playing, providing feedback, etc. The purpose will be to extinguish old behaviors, such as avoiding personal interaction, withdrawing from emotional communication, or giving pat responses, and reinforcing new behaviors, such as listening actively, soliciting thoughts and feelings, and giving accurate feedback..

Whatever the strategies may be for changing habits, the intent should be reflected clearly, as always, in the instructional objectives.

3. Should the learner develop a particular moral viewpoint toward the job or tasks for which he is being trained?

Training is typically more than preparing people to perform tasks. It is also a socialization process. Whether an instructor is aware of it or not, he or she transmits to the learner many of his or her own attitudes about the job being taught.

The evaluator should prompt the trainer to consider the socialization dimension of his or her course or program. The Armed Forces provide the clearest example of socialization through training. Consider the extent to which the individual's behavior is shaped during basic training or advanced specialty training. Practically every dimension of daily living is subject to close supervision during the training process and almost every human activity is ritualized—even eating and personal grooming. Most of this regimentation is introduced to ensure order, obedience, predictable and effective responses to danger, and high morale.

In years past, a similar if not nearly so uniform and intense a socialization process took place at the federal government's Social Security Administration. All new personnel attended orientation training, which was geared not only to provide useful information about the agency but also to enlist the personal commitment of the new worker to the high goals of the program. Indeed, the Social Security administration, under the direction of its most distinguished commissioner, Robert Ball, exuded a palpable *esprit de corps* that was exceptional for any level of governmental service.

Of course, training can only plant the seeds of socialization. It must find fertile soil in the everyday life of the organization. Therefore, the trainer must be realistic when considering the possibilities. Yet, the potential is well worth exploring. And again, formulating objectives for this aspect of attitudinal development is difficult, though not impossible. Nor must it be relegated to orientation training. One objective which would be appropriate for much of the technical training at any social service agency is the following:

> *The learner consistently acts in a manner that demonstrates concern for the welfare of the client when dealing with complex or troublesome claims cases.*

The concern may be demonstrated through persistence in difficult tasks and individual and team efforts to find solutions to casework problems as opposed to automatically referring difficult cases to a backlog of unfinished cases.

People in service occupations generally wish to provide quality service, but in many cases they need a great deal of help in learning how to provide it. Much of that help can come by way of demonstrating commitment through role modeling and providing training opportunities for the learner to express that commitment. Strategies such as these may be prompted by instructional objectives which call for socialization in terms of specific behavior or job performance.

Instructional Objectives Checklist

The preceding questions and the narrative accompanying them are not meant to be all-inclusive. Rather, they are starting points and reference points for the evaluator as he or she assesses the trainer's objectives for the learner. The following checklist is provided as a ready reference for attending to these assessment questions.

Instructional Objectives Evaluation Checklist

Information Objectives	Question not applicable	Question adequately addressed in objectives	Improvement recommended*
1. Is the information to be learned clearly defined?			
2. Is the information based on a current training needs analysis or occupational analysis?			
3. Is it necessary for the learner to memorize the details of information or is it sufficient to be able to readily access information?			
4. Is some information more crucial than other information?			
Intellectual Skill Objectives			
1. Is the learner required to learn new concepts or procedures?			
2. What are the standards for learner performance?			
3. Will the job require the learner to use particular reference or research skills?			
4. Must human interaction skills be developed as partial preparation for the job?			
Motor Skill Objectives			
1. Is the learner required to learn any physical tasks?			

	Question not applicable	Question adequately addressed in objectives	Improvement recommended*
2. Do the motor skills require a specific mastery level?			
3. Are there safety procedures or precautions to be learned?			
4. Can and should the motor skills be practiced in any actual or simulated situation?			

Attitude Objectives

1. Are there any concerns about the learner's attitude toward the topic of training?			
2. Are there old habits that need to be extinguished and new habits that require reinforcement?			
3. Should the learner develop a particular moral viewpoint toward the job or tasks for which he is being trained?			

---

*Where improvement is recommended, the evaluator should attach notes which describe the essence of his or her analysis and the nature of the recommendations.

These questions have been recommended as a guide for the evaluator. They are neither mandatory nor exhaustive. However, if they can be answered satisfactorily, the evaluator is likely to have all the information he or she requires to judge whether or not the trainer's objectives for the learner accurately and fully reflect the purposes of training.

This is the first major task of the evaluator, and it is an extremely important one. After all, no matter how well the learner masters what is offered him or her, if the information, skills and attitudes which training addresses are inappropriate or inadequate in meeting the purposes of training, the training has failed.

> **Review of Progress**
>
> **Evaluator Task #1: Assess the appropriateness and adequacy of instructional objectives.**
>
> Enabling Skills:
> - Ability to classify statements as performance or non-performance.
> - Ability to identify performance objectives as dealing with information, intellectual skills, motor skills or attitude.
> - Ability to ask appropriate questions regarding the purposes of training.

References

Assessing training needs
Brown, F. Gerald and Wedel, Kenneth R. *Assessing training needs.* Washington, D.C.: National Training and Development Service Press, 1974.
Johnson, Richard B. Determining training needs. In R. Craig and L. Bittel (Eds.), *Training and Development Handbook,* Chapter 2. New York: McGraw-Hill, 1967.

Occupational Analysis
Christal, R.E. *The United States Airforce Occupational Research Project.* Lackland AFB: Airforce Human Resources Laboratory, January 1974. (Report No. AFHRL-TR-73-75)
Driskill, Walter E. Occupational analysis in the United States Airforce. Paper presented at the National Symposium on Task Analysis/Inventories, Ohio State University, Columbus, Ohio, November 18, 1975. [Dr. Driskill's paper may be obtained by written request from the following address: U.S. Airforce Occupational Measurement Center, USASOMC/OMY, Randolph AFB, TX 78150.]

Answers to Module 1 Test

3, 4, 6, 9, 10, 14 and 15.

Answers to Module 2 Test

1.	MS	11.	MS
2.	IS	12.	IS
3.	MS	13.	A
4.	I	14.	I
5.	A	15.	I
6.	IS	16.	MS
7.	I	17.	IS
8.	A	18.	A
9.	IS	19.	MS
10.	I	20.	IS

Chapter 3

What Did They Really Learn?

Through years of exposure in school, trainers are familiar with standard testing formats—true and false, matching, multiple choice, fill-in and essay.

Of course, exposure never guarantees competence, so it is likely that unless the trainer has received specific instruction in test construction, his or her test items and test formats will bear improvement. The evaluator should be able to give the trainer critical feedback on tests he or she has constructed (or borrowed) in order to assess learner achievement as a result of instruction.

However, we will not attempt to address all the specifics of test construction since it would require a full volume of text and has been adequately treated elsewhere. The reader will find Charles Denova's *Test Construction for Training Evaluation* a particularly useful text in preparing tests for adult learners. It covers all standard test formats as well as performance testing. We will concentrate on the effective use of one generic type of testing that is by and large the most appropriate for training programs— *criterion-referenced testing*. As a result of this chapter, the reader should be able to judge the fundamental adequacy of the tests trainers have constructed or selected to administer to the learner. He or she should also be able to help the trainer improve his or her use of tests for making decisions about the learner and the instruction.

Criterion-Referenced Testing

A criterion-referenced test (CRT) is one in which responses are assessed according to specific criteria or set standards. These criteria or standards are the *references* the examiner uses in judging the adequacy of the learner's responses.

An example of a CRT with set standards is a typical written driver's exam. The test has been constructed to cover the important rules of the road, and the applicant is required to achieve a minimal score (perhaps 70 percent). That minimal percentage of correct responses is the standard.

Other CRTs have many criteria which the test-taker must meet in order to "pass" or demonstrate mastery. For example, consider a group of trainees learning how to conduct client interviews as preparation for their jobs as case workers. The trainer wishes to test each learner on his or ability to perform the complex task of properly interviewing a client.

In order to construct a suitable test of that performance, the trainer must identify the criteria for successful job performance. He or she may derive something like the following:

- The client is set at ease.
- Questions are posed in a non-threatening way.
- Probing is conducted where necessary.
- All essential information is elicited.
- All essential information is fully and accurately recorded.
- The interviewer maintains a professional demeanor.
- Correct procedural information is given to the client in a manner the client can understand.

The trainer may not yet be able to expose the learner to a real client, but he or she can use individuals who can effectively role-play clients. The trainer can observe the learner interviewing the client-substitutes and can rate his or her performance on the seven criteria which comprise successful performance.

If the learner fails to satisfy one or more criteria, he or she can be told or shown specifically what factor in the performance needs improvement. Ideally, each learner should continue to receive instruction or practice with feedback until he or she meets all the criteria for successful performance.

How much more accurately does this CRT assess the learner's ability to actually perform a complex task than would a paper and pencil test which requires the learner simply to describe or identify the elements of good interviewing? Perhaps learners should be able to describe them, but if they can't apply them as well, their training has fallen short.

Using CRTs for the Major Types of Learning

Criterion-referenced testing is particularly appropriate for most skills instruction—typing, computer programming, welding or operating a weapons system. Wherever we can observe or measure with reasonable reliability, we can test to criteria. At the same time, CRT is applicable to information learning and attitude learning as well. Let's consider examples for each of the major types of human learning as we might find them within the scope of one job—that of a railroad brakeman. The brakeman must learn a well-defined body of information as well as several motor skills and intellectual skills and attitudes in order to adequately and safely perform each of his or her major job functions. We will consider only the job function of coupling and uncoupling cars for purposes of illustration. Let's first look at the four types of human learning as reflected in the performance objectives for that function.

Information Objectives
1. Correctly identify and name the parts of the coupler.
2. Identify the different positions of the coupler.
3. Explain the use of all associated equipment in coupling and uncoupling cars.

4. Recite the rules from the brakeman's manual which pertain to coupling and uncoupling cars.

5. Describe the key differences between positioning a regular coupler and a long-shank coupler between cars and locomotives.

6. State the safety precautions unique to raising bridgeplates on piggyback cars.

Intellectual Skill Objectives

1. Identify equipment that requires replacement or repair.

2. Determine whether cars are adequately positioned for coupling.

3. Given the different positions of the coupler, indicate the proper sequence of steps for coupling or uncoupling.

Motor Skill Objectives

1. Demonstrate the proper way to couple cars.

2. Demonstrate the proper way to uncouple standing cars.

3. Demonstrate the proper position for holding the lift lever and signaling movement in both directions when uncoupling.

4. Demonstrate the proper way to replace a knuckle.

5. Demonstrate uncoupling from a moving car on a hump.

6. Demonstrate uncoupling from a moving car during flat switching.

Attitude Objectives

1. Choose to follow all safety procedures with consistency and deliberateness.

2. Choose to report defective equipment rather than use it.

Each of these instructional objectives provides a *reference* for testing the learner, i.e., it provides basic information for designing test situations which will enable us to observe whether the learner can actually perform those tasks he or she is taught.

A CRT Based on Instructional Objectives

One of the most agonizing problems railroads face is the high rate and seriousness of injury to railroad equipment-handling personnel, especially brakemen. Besides other potentially dangerous tasks, the brakeman is regularly called on to work between locomotives and cars which weigh several tons and which may crush the worker in a single unanticipated jolt from an engine if all safety precautions have not been taken.

As a measure against injury, railroads have developed comprehensive operational safety manuals which specify in detail exactly how an equipment handler should perform each of his or her tasks. As you will see from the following example, safety precautions are built into job performance, thus becoming part of the criteria for judging whether performance is adquate. Note that it coincides with the first motor skill objective given above.

Task: Positioning Coupler Between Cars or Locomotives
1. Look and listen to determine that car movement has stopped and slack has been adjusted.
2. Notify foreman or engineer that you are going to step between cars.
3. Look in both directions for moving equipment on or about tracks.
4. Step over rail, observing placement of feet to ensure secure footing (DO NOT position yourself in front of couplers).
5. Position yourself inside the rail, facing side of coupler.
6. Maintain balance and grasp couplers with both hands.
7. Slowly push or pull coupler to desired position (if unable to position coupler, seek assistance).
8. Step over rail, observing area where feet are placed to ensure secure footing.
9. Keep alert for unexpected movement and look and listen for equipment moving on adjacent track.

These procedures may appear overly detailed to someone not familiar with the accidents which have occured in the car-coupling process, but it is essential that they be learned by the apprentice exactly as prescribed. Here the trainer may not be satisfied with 80 percent accuracy in performance since several steps in the procedure, if not adequately performed, could result in serious injury or death. It is not enough for the apprentice brakeman to successfully couple the cars. Any step left out or performed inadequately means the performance has failed to meet the criteria.

Once we know precisely what the learner should be able to do, our next concern is over how we should go about testing him or her. A good rule to start with is the following: *Create a test that is as close to actual job performance as possible.* In the case of training the apprentice brakeman on the task of coupling and uncoupling cars, we can start by considering how close to actual job performance we can get. We may discover that it is overly inconvenient and expensive to interfere with normal train yard operations. Therefore, we tentatively rule out testing under actual working conditions. However, we discover that we may appropriate a few locomotives and several cars for training purposes as well as a spur of track that is seldom used for normal yard operations.

These conditions will allow us to simulate actual operating procedures with reasonable fidelity, and they allow us to stop a procedure at any point to give useful feedback to the apprentice on his performance, something we could not do so readily during actual working conditions.

Format for Test Development

The following format is simply a way of displaying the logical progression from instructional objectives to test situation and test items. If a trainer cannot show that his or her tests accurately reflect the objectives or that he or she judges performance according to specific criteria, the evaluator has an opportunity to lend considerable help. With the following format as a reference, he or she can review the instructional objectives with the trainer and prompt the trainer to develop performance criteria and devise test situations that come as close as possible to matching actual job performance.

Criterion-Referenced Test Worksheet

Objectives	Criteria	Test Situation
Motor Skill #1 Demonstrate the proper way to couple cars.	1. Look and listen 2. Notify foreman 3. Look in both 4. Step over rail 5. Position yourself 6. Maintain balance 7. Slowly push 8. Step over rail 9. Keep alert	Personnel: engineer, foreman and trainer. Equipment: locomotive and two cars. Location: track spur 49. Procedure: apprentices take turns positioning couplers; foreman provides feedback and trainer records whether each has mastered task.

Format for Test Evaluation

As you can see, the test worksheet shown above is primarily for the trainer's use in developing his or her tests. However, the evaluator may wish to record his or her own analysis of the trainer's tests. The following format may be appropriate.

Test Evaluation Checklist

Objectives	Yes	No	Comments
1. Objective stated in performance terms.			
2. Performance criteria are adequate.			

Test Situation
3. Performance is under actual work conditions.
4. Performance is under simulated conditions.
5. Substitution made for required performance.
*6. Test situation requires modification.

*In those cases where a test situation or test item needs to be modified or totally reconstructed, the evaluator may wish to attach a description of his or her analysis and recommendations to the form.

The Test Evaluation Checklist is relatively easy for the evaluator to fill in once he or she has access to the information called for by the Criterion-Referenced Test Worksheet. Remember that the CRT Worksheet calls for the trainer to lay out the logical progression of thought behind his or her methods of testing. The evaluator can then judge whether his or her own criteria have been met with the help of the Test Evaluation Checklist.

Let's briefly consider each item on the checklist:

1. *Objectives stated in performance terms.* The only way to be certain a given test is appropriate is to know what the learner is supposed to be able to do as a result of instruction. That requirement brings us back to performance objectives. The more specific and clear the objectives, the clearer the implications for testing. Where objectives are vague or only implicit in the instruction, the evaluator should ask questions such as those given in Chapter 2 to elicit as full an understanding as possible of the major purposes of training. From that understanding, performance objectives can be constructed at least tentatively so that the evaluator has an objective reference against which to measure all that follows in the way of instruction and testing.

2. *Performance criteria are adequate.* Just as the evaluator may perform a useful service in prompting and guiding the trainer in the formulation of clear performance objectives for instruction, so too with respect to performance criteria. A useful question to pose is: "How can you distinguish between acceptable and unacceptable performance?" Speed, accuracy, timeliness and responsiveness to change in the work environment are common criteria, but only a close examination of job performance will yield a fully satisfactory set of criteria, as it did for the brakeman's job tasks.

3. *Performance is under actual work conditions.* This means that the trainer has been able to arrange for the learner to be tested in a real work setting. At first, testing on the job may appear awkward and difficult to administer. However, considering the importance of near flawless performance in some occupations, on-the-job testing may be worth the inconvenience.

Consider police work. Normally a new police officer is assigned to a senior partner who is expected to "bring the rookie officer along." A training program could incorporate this first stage of actual job performance by providing the senior partner with checksheets on the performance of new officers. The senior partner would be asked not to "rate" the new officer but to identify areas of performance for which further training would be useful. If additional training is offered in the spirit of continual professional development as opposed to remedial work, it should meet with reasonably positive reception.

4. *Performance is under simulated conditions.* Here the trainer has found a way to simulate actual job performance. The evaluator must judge whether the simulation needs to be improved in order for the learner to make successful transition from simulation to the actual job.

For example, suppose a simulation exercise is used to test the ability of managers to make sound decisions in a timely manner. Typically, managers must make decisions in the absence of complete information. Therefore, a simulation in which all pertinent information is supplied for decision making is not an accurate one.

5. *Substitution made for required performance.* In this case, the trainer has not been able to simulate actual job performance but has accepted some other performance in its place, e.g., accepting a written description of how to design a security system as evidence of the ability to actually construct one. It is likely that where substitutions are made for required performance, some substantial improvement can be made in testing. It is also likely that the trainer may be clearly cognizant of his or her test's shortcomings but has not received the necessary support from the organization to construct the required simulations.

The evaluator may sometimes be able to bridge communication gaps the trainer cannot by virture of his or her role and relationship to decision makers in the organization. Frequently, the evaluator's job is to provide feedback to management as well as to the trainer, and management's role in providing necessary support for training is an appropriate subject for the evaluator's analysis.

6. *Test situation requires modification.* Based upon the evaluator's analysis for each of the preceding items, he or she may decide that one or more of the test situations require modification, or he or she may have uncovered course objectives which have not been tested for in any manner.

It is necessary and perhaps sufficient to describe why a given test situation as presently constructed is inadequate. However, the evaluator can be of significant help to the trainer by also projecting ideas about how the test situations can be made more effective or by posing questions which prompt the trainer to reflect upon the fundamentals:
a. What do the objectives call for?
b. What are the performance criteria (or what should they be), i.e., what distinguishes adequate from inadequate job performance?
c. How can the performance be tested in an actual situation or an effectively simulated situation?

CRT's as Feedback

In addition to determining the adequacy of the trainer's tests for checking or measuring learner performance, the evaluator should also study the trainer's use of the information which his or her tests yield. Basically, the trainer may use the information for three purposes:

1. To give the learner feedback which will assist him in maintaining or modifying his or her performance.

2. To certify the learner as "competent," i.e., that he or she has sufficiently mastered the learning to graduate from instruction...or to screen the learner out of the instructional process as insufficiently qualified or prepared for the job.

3. To modify instruction so it becomes more efficient and effective in meeting the needs of the learner and the requirements of the job.

Giving the Learner Feedback

Feedback is of vital importance to learning. In some cases, the learner can directly observe and judge the effectiveness of his performance with no assistance, as perhaps in learning to prepare food. However, some form of feedback from the instructor is normally required in order that the learner be able to improve performance during the course of training. A most graphic example of feedback as a necessary component of instruction is target-marking. After a weapon is fired, a target is marked in a highly visible manner so that the learner can see exactly where his shots impacted. Without this feedback, accuracy would be almost impossible to attain.

In light of the learner's need for feedback to improve performance, we can state the following principles:

1. Frequent testing is generally preferable to infrequent or no testing.

2. The more detailed a critique of performance the trainer can provide through the test, the more useful will the test be to the learner.

3. The sooner the feedback is given after the test is taken, the more useful it will be to the learner.

Feedback can be given regularly by the trainer without formal testing. It doesn't matter whether the trainer considers this part of his or her instructional activities for the learner or part of his or her testing for learning. What matters is that the learner be given accurate and timely feedback to the degree he or she requires it to adequately learn his or her tasks. The Evaluator Checklist on Trainer's Feedback to the Learner (below) is provided as a way for the evaluator to gauge the trainer's treatment of each major performance objective.

Evaluator Checklist on
Trainer's Feedback to the Learner

Performance Objective:

Informal or instructional feedback to the learner is

_____ unnecessary

_____ useful

_____ necessary

Test feedback to the learner is

_____ unnecessary

_____ useful

_____ necessary

Informal or instructional feedback is presently

_____ not provided

_____ insufficient

_____ sufficient

Test feedback is presently

_____ unnecessary

_____ useful

_____ necessary

Recommendations for improvement:

Certifying the Learner as Competent

As noted in Chapter 2, no one fails entry-level training in many organizations. Yet job performance is frequently rated as unsatisfactory. Of course, insufficient training or unqualified personnel are not the sole reasons for poor performance, but they are possible causes. And it is reasonable to assume that if personnel come to the job unable to perform at a minimal level of competence, then either the training or the candidate selection process (or both) are inadequate.

Candidate selection is normally beyond the scope of the trainer's function. He or she must take whomever he or she is given to train. However, the trainer is in a unique position to provide useful feedback to those who select the candidates. Trainers should know what skills, knowledge and attitudes are required for successful job performance and they should be able to develop, over time, a baseline profile they believe a candidate must possess to achieve minimal competence through training. For example, they may find that a 10th-grade reading level is a prerequisite for comprehending service manuals which the learner is required to use as a job reference.

At the same time, trainers must be prepared to defend their training as an effective and efficient preparation for job performance. Moreover, their tests must accurately reflect job performance. There have been several instances within the last decade of candidates failing entry-level training programs and subsequently being denied entry into jobs. Some of these candidates have sued in court, claiming training tests to be essentially irrelevant to actual job performance. Generally, where training has been clearly based upon performance objectives and tests have been criterion-referenced, claimants have been denied redress by the courts.

Therefore, it behooves the evaluator to learn what the policy is regarding the use of training for screening job candidates. For the good of the organization and in ultimate fairness to all candidates, reasonable minimal criteria should be set for performance on tests given during or at the conclusion of training whenever the candidate is to enter a job in which a similar minimal performance level must be met. To ignore minimal criteria where it is critical to satisfactory job performance is to perform a disservice both to the organization and to its clients.

The evaluator can assist the trainer in establishing defensible and useful minimal performance criteria by encouraging him or her to carry out the analysis suggested by the form below.

Analysis of Minimal Performance Criteria

Job: Clerk-typist   Training: Clerk-typist basic course.

Criteria for minimal job performance	Corresponding instructional objectives	Corresponding tests	Corresponding instruction
1. 50 words per minute with no more than 2 errors per 250 words.	Learner will be able to type at least 50 WPM with no more than 2 errors per 250 words while copying typical office correspondence.	Daily typing drills; peer-evaluated exercises; formal tests with several chances to meet criteria.	Demonstration and drill; individual feedback on exercises given by instructor; peer feedback on exercises; tests are reviewed afterward for identification of problems.
2. Take phone calls; route to appropriate persons; take messages with sufficient information for return call.	None.	None.	None.

The samples shown in the form above reveal that, while the critical skill of typing is adequately covered in the training, the skill of handling incoming calls for office personnel is not treated at all. This is a common omission which, like others, occurs when minimal performance standards or criteria have either not been developed for a job or have not been conveyed to the trainer.

By obtaining the criteria for minimal job performance, a trainer is in a position to establish his or her own minimal criteria for performance on tests. That doesn't mean he or she can't gear instruction for performance above the minimum level, only that he or she will accept performance at, but not below, the minimum. His or her own objective, for example, may be to bring the class of clerk-typists as a whole to a level of 80 words per minute with accuracy. But he or she will accept from any given learner as little as 50 words per minute with accuracy.

Modify Instruction

Robert Stake has drawn a useful distinction between two basic ways of planning and conducting research and has suggested that these distinctions apply to training and education as well. The distinction is between rationalism and empiricism. According to the rationalist, we should think first, plan ahead, then act and test. According to the empiricist, we should act first, observe, build up a backlog of experience, then infer. The rationalist would have us invest more in planning; the empiricist would have us invest more in experience.

Stake describes teachers as predominantly empiricists. Most trainers are empiricists by intellectual bent, preferring to plan sketchily and tentatively, ready to scrap one strategy for another as they get to know the learner and his or her needs. It is well that most trainers are empirical by bent. After all, it is they who must ultimately find a workable strategy for bringing the learner and that which is to be learned together effectively. Instructional design is far from being an exact science, despite its cast of technological sophistication, so the trainer must be able to modify, abandon and experiment with all manner of instructional strategy.

However, this intellectual bent toward empiricism does not necessarily guarantee that the trainer will profitably use all the feedback at his or her disposal to modify instruction. The trainer usually prefers qualitative feedback to quantitative. That means he or she is more apt to alter instruction if he or she senses the learner is becoming confused or bored than if the learner performs poorly on a test.

The evaluator can assist the trainer to review test results for a reason other than assessing whether the learner has learned, i.e., whether the instruction has been effective. This is rarely an easy question to answer, for learning is the product of combined effort on the part of learner *and* instructor. However, as a rough rule of thumb, if the majority or even a large minority of learners have failed to learn, then the instruction has fallen short. This presumes a good faith effort on the part of most learners.

In practice, trainers must decide for themselves what constitutes an acceptable level of learner failure. The evaluator can at least show them a simple way of determining where this instruction is most vulnerable by focusing on test results. A sample is shown below. (A more sophisticated method of identifying poor test items or inadequate instruction can be found in Norman E. Gronlund's widely used text, *Constructing Achievement Tests,* 3rd Ed., Prentice Hall, Inc., Englewood Cliffs, N.J., 1982.)

Test Items	% Learners with Correct Responses	Instruction Needs Review
1. Remove baffle without damaging plating.	100%	No
2. Bore cylindar walls within tolerances.	65%	Yes
3. Rewire circuitry in correct pattern.	85%	No
4. Estimate repair costs.	95%	No
5. Order appropriate parts.	100%	No
6. Detect defective switches.	40%	Yes
7. Replace switches with duplicates.	30%	Yes

Did They Really Need the Training?

Much of what has been said thus far about testing presumes that the learners do not already possess the information, skills or attitudes we wish to teach them. For much entry-level training, this is a reasonable assumption. We don't expect to find people entering the apprentice phase of a craft or profession already in full command of the necessary knowledge and skills, whether in welding, claims processing, air traffic control, railroad equipment handling or any other technical job. Thus, when we ask the central question of this chapter—"What have they really learned?"—we presume that what they have learned is what they are able to demonstrate on the criterion-referenced tests taken during or at the conclusion of training.

Not all training, however, is technical entry-level for basic job performance. Nor should we always assume that the learner comes to training as yet unable to meet instructional objectives. We considered in Chapter 2 an example of training in which physicians and medical researchers learned how to handle radioactive isotopes. You may recall we discovered the problem was not that participants didn't know what the safety procedures were but that they had chosen not to employ them because the procedures were inconvenient—they got in the way of carrying out lab work in the most efficient and comfortable manner.

The team which evaluated this training was led to its discovery in part through a pretesting of the course participants. Just prior to the first lecture/demonstration, the training course manager handed out a short test. The evaluators had prompted the course manager to select a small but representative sample of test items from his final exam to give to the participants at the start of the course. From the 65-item exam, he selected eight for the pre-test (approximately a 12 percent sample). They comprised a reasonably accurate representation of subject matter and test item complexity.

To the surprise of the course manager, as many as one third of the participants scored 75 percent or better on this pre-test (70 percent was the standard for passing the final exam). This suggested that several course participants did not need much of the instructional package as it was then constituted.

Upon discovering this, the evaluators began questioning participants about their motives for taking the training. It turned out that the training was a prerequisite for licensing and a license was necessary for ordering and using radioactive isotopes. Thus, anyone who wished to work with such isotopes had to take the course regardless of their need for the instruction.

The evaluators ultimately made recommendations for restructuring the course to better meet the varying needs of participants. The point is that some sort of diagnostic testing for training needs may be in order wherever you cannot assume uniform lack of job preparedness on the part of the learner.

What Do Diagnostic Tests Look Like?

A diagnostic test can look much like a test given during or at the conclusion of training—true-false, multiple-choice, essay or performance. However, its actual composition should be determined by its purpose. For example, suppose we are directed to develop basic supervisory training for a large organization's first-line supervisors. We may wish to find out how most supervisors perform by the time they get to training in a number of areas: delegating work, delegating authority and responsibility, employee rights, methods of employee development, maintaining open communications and others.

We may find that a few key test situations will give us a good estimate of the level of knowledge or competence held by potential trainees in each major area of learning. For example, we may establish a "diagnostic center" or "assessment center" where we put the supervisor through a brief set of paper exercises and simulations before training. The following test situations are illustrative.

1. *Paper exercise*—a problem of employee performance being below an acceptable level is delineated for the supervisor. The problem is formulated to make employee development the key to the appropriate supervisory response. The supervisor's knowledge of employee development possibilities and his or her ability to apply employee development principles are assessed from his or her response to the hypothetical problem.

2. *Paper exercise*—a description of a harried supervisor who tries to do everything himself or herself is presented for response. The description is formulated to make delegation of work and responsibility the key to the appropriate supervisory response. The supervisor's ability to apply the principles of delegation are assessed from his or her response.

3. *Simulation*—confidential communications are arranged in which the supervisor must deal verbally with "employees" who bring a variety of needs and frustrations to the supervisor. The supervisor's understanding of employee rights and his or her ability to maintain open communications are assessed from this simulation.

From the supervisor's responses to the diagnostic testing done in the center, the trainer can observe the range of abilities already possessed by supervisors as well as their greatest areas of deficiency. These responses allow the trainer to tailor instruction to some degree so that a great deal of time and energy are not spent on skill development where skills already meet criteria. Rather, instruction can be focused primarily on those areas in which knowledge and skill development are clearly needed.

The evaluator may wish to recommend the format shown below for the trainer's use in performing diagnosis before conducting training. As previous formats were suggested for the trainer's use, Diagnosis of Learner Strengths and Deficiencies is designed to help the trainer systematically review his instructional plans for possible improvement. By reviewing the information displayed in this format, the evaluator is in a good position to form a more complete and satisfactory answer to the question—"What did they really learn?"—for he or she will know what the learner already possessed by way of information, skills and attitude before he or she entered the training. He or she will also be able to judge how well the trainer has planned in tailoring instruction to account for specific learner strengths and deficiencies.

Diagnosis of Learner Strengths and Deficiencies

Objective	Criteria for Performance	Diagnosis of Learner Needs	Instructional Implications
Supervisor will be able to demonstrate open communications in stressful situations.	1. Does not avoid communication. 2. Seeks communication where employee appears to be having difficulty emotionally or in his or her work. 3. Clarifies employee discourse through questioning. 4. Shows genuine interest. 5. Supplies accurate feedback, even when unpleasant.	Most supervisors responded in way that shows: 1. They don't avoid communication per se. 2. They don't clarify employee discourse. 3. They don't provide useful feedback, especially when it should contain information unpleasant for employee to hear.	Emphasis should be increased on simulated one-on-one communications to build supervisors' capabilities and willingness to: 1. Come to grips with the real problem 2. Give useful feedback to the employee, even when the message is unpleasant.

Summary

Testing is an essential component of training. It is often neglected because the trainer is not sufficiently adept at constructing test items and test situations which adequately sample learner performance. The evaluator, even if he or she is not adept at test construction, can provide the trainer with useful guidance in the way of questions, suggestions and formats, such as those provided in this chapter. He or she can also advise the trainer in the use of diagnostic tests where they are useful for purposes of adjusting instructional plans to best meet learner needs.

Review of Progress

Evaluator Task #2: Assess the appropriateness and adequacy of test instruments, test situations and the use of test results for training.

Enabling Skills:
- Ability to prescribe performance criteria for instructional objectives.

- Ability to prescribe test items and test situations based upon instructional objectives and performance criteria.

- Ability to prescribe test items and test situations for purposes of diagnosing learner needs, providing feedback on learner performance, certifying the learner as competent and modifying instruction.

Reference

Stake, R.E. *Language, rationality, and assessment.* In D.A. Payne (Ed.), Curriculum evaluation. Lexington, Mass: D.C. Heath & Co., 1974.

Chapter 4

How Well Did We Execute?

We have emphasized planning as a major key to achieving effective training results. Now we turn to the subject of implementation or execution, for it is also essential to achieving effective results. The focus of this chapter is on instructional strategy with the intent that the reader be able to judge the effectiveness of a trainer's strategy for bringing the learner up to performance criteria. He or she should also be able to judge how effective the trainer is in conducting the actual events of instruction.

Instructional Strategy

An instructional strategy is a plan of execution—the trainer's plan for accomplishing his or her instructional objectives. As such, it includes all the components of instruction that directly affect the learner: instructor activities, learner activities, instructional material, equipment and physical environment. The evaluator should be aware of each of these components as he or she studies the trainer's instructional strategies to determine their adequacy.

How can we determine in theory whether an instructional strategy will work effectively? We cannot with absolute certainty. After all, there may be things about the instructor, the learner, the instructional material, the equipment or the environment that will affect the learner's ability to achieve in ways we will not have anticipated. For example, an instructor who is prepared to teach advanced composition skills may discover with the first writing assignment results that many of his or her students lack the prerequisite skills for the intended level of learner performance.

However, while we cannot be certain that an instructional strategy will work effectively, we can look for certain properties which characterize effective strategies. One of the most systematic and convenient ways of doing that is by checking a given strategy against a model. Several have been proposed in the educational and training literature for varying instructional purposes, but offered here is a generic model designed to fit most training situations.

The model, Model of Instruction for Training (MIT), is displayed and described below. It is offered as a guide rather than a prescription for thorough instructional planning. Therefore, the evaluator should use it to raise questions about the trainer's strategies and offer suggestions rather than apply it too strictly.

Model of Instruction for Training (MIT)

Principles	Methods
1. Prepare the learner.	1.1 Dramatize purpose and importance of subject matter. 1.2 Review previous learning. 1.3 Provide framework for understanding. 1.4 Trigger curiosity.
2. Present stimuli.	2.1 Verbal communication. 2.2 Mediated communication. 2.3 Deductive approach. 2.4 Inductive approach. 2.5 Part to whole approach. 2.6 Whole to part approach 2.7 Modeling
3. Evoke learning.	3.1 Memorization. 3.2 Concept formation. 3.3 Rule learning. 3.4 Attitude development.
4. Provide feedback.	4.1 Verbal feedback. 4.2 Performance feedback. 4.3 Reinforcement.
5. Test performance.	5.1 Actual performance. 5.2 Simulation. 5.3 Substitution.
6. Follow-through.	6.1 Overlearning. 6.2 Certification. 6.3 Prescription.

1. PREPARE THE LEARNER.

1.1 Dramatize purpose and importance of subject matter.

One way to evoke a sense of willingness in the learner to attend carefully to instruction is by dramatizing the purpose and importance of the subject matter. There are a variety of ways to do this. One, for example, is to illustrate what would occur or what does occur as a result of not possessing the appropriate knowledge or skills.

A practical instance of this method in use is a class for data technicians on the proper procedure for storing data. The trainer dramatizes the purpose and importance of this procedure by showing how minutes, even hours, of data entry can be lost through failure to systematically enter into storage what has been typed onto the terminal.

1.2 Review previous learning.

Another way to prepare the learner is by briefly reviewing material which he or she has already learned and which bears close relevance to the subject matter at hand. For example, the trainer of brakeman apprentices might review what the learner had learned about manual hand brakes before introducing power hand brakes, since most of the basic procedures and safety precautions for operating manual hand brakes apply equally to the power hand brakes.

In essence, by reviewing previous learning, the trainer helps the learner transfer his or her knowledge or skill from one application to another.

1.3 Provide framework for understanding.

This technique is also meant to assist the learner to grasp the information or develop the skill at hand. But unlike reviewing previous learning, the purpose here is to provide a comprehensive picture for the learner which will help him or her to organize the information or skill in an orderly and efficient manner. Prominent psychologist David Ausubel has called this framework for understanding an "advanced organizer," since it offers the learner a conceptual scheme for fitting together all that follows into a meaningful whole. Ausubel considers it the most efficient way of presenting large bodies of informatin to the learner.

Thus, for example, the trainer who intends to describe and demonstrate the several types of signals used in railroading might first list the major categories of signals—fuses, flags, hand signals, lights, engine warning signals, etc.—and then subsume each signal he or she will demonstrate under one of the categories. This framework assists the learner to organize the information as he or she internalizes it.

1.4 Trigger curiosity.

This technique can be very effective though it is not always easy to devise. It consists of creating a question or a set of questions in the learner's mind—questions for which he or she wants answers. For example: "What do you suppose would happen if you threw a hand switch the wrong way in front of an engine traveling 15 miles per hour?" Speculation about derailment, damage to equipment and injury to personnel would ensue. This could be used as an introduction to switching procedures in the railroad yard. It would capture initial interest because it triggers the learner's curiosity about the serious implications of a mistake he or she could easily make.

2. PRESENT STIMULI.

2.1 Verbal communication.

The most natural, intuitive way to convey information is through verbal expression. Yet, we must consider its relative limitations and strengths before we lean too heavily upon it for instructional purposes. Its limitations are many:

a. The learner cannot control the flow of input in order to study and absorb it at his or her own pace.

b. The learner must rely almost solely upon his listening skills; yet we know that many people are better visual learners than verbal.

c. Clarity and accuracy of messages can suffer significantly in verbal communication due to the inherent limitations of the speaker who may be composing the communication as he or she goes along.

d. Skills development is normally difficult to induce verbally. At best, verbal communication serves as a guide and supplement to an actual demonstration of performance.

At the same time, verbal communication possesses some unique strengths:

a. A live speaker can convey nuances of meaning through voice inflection, gesture and facial expression which are extremely difficult to approximate in other communication modes.

b. It is the simplest mode of communication to plan for (no equipment is required).

c. It can fully capture the listener's attention under the right conditions. (Story telling remains a popular art, despite how sophisticated the entertainment media have become.)

d. It can be easily altered to meet rapidly changing conditions in the training situation.

Taken together, the strengths and limitations of verbal communication suggest that the trainer not rely upon it too heavily as a vehicle for large bodies of information or for skill development. Rather, it is best used as a way of preparing the learner (questions, stories and dramatizations of the subject's importance) and of speaking to particular concerns the learner may have as he or she interacts with the instruction. Verbal communication can be used effectively in making a transition from one learning activity to another and as a means of helping the learner put activities into a meaningful framework of understanding.

2.2 Mediated communication.

Mediated communication is any communication that is transmitted partially or totally through some form other than direct human voice. Partial mediators are such things as overhead projectors, chalkboards and flip charts. They provide a visual dimension which complements the verbal message of the trainer. Total mediators are tapes, films and programmed texts designed for the learner's use without need of intermittent communication with the instructor.

Mediated instruction should be considered in some form wherever a large body of information must be conveyed to the learner. Its basic strengths are the following:

a. Messages can be carefully designed for accuracy and clarity.

b. The learner can often control the flow of information, e.g., by stopping a tape or rereading a page.

c. Messages can be structured for more effective assimilation by the learner, e.g., through categorizing information into convenient headings and sub-headings.

d. Learners who have difficulty with verbal communication can use their visual skills to compensate.

A trainer needs to realize that using media will not automatically improve instruction. In fact, poorly developed mediated instruction can confuse a learner more than stricly verbal communication. Consider the common practice of placing too much information on overhead transparencies. Transparencies should be used to help the learner organize information, not to convey large bodies of information.

Tapes and films are often produced to serve a general learning audience. As such, they may only partially or indirectly pertain to a specific instruction objective. Therefore, the trainer needs to provide some pointed verbal communication before and after (and perhaps during) the tape or film to help the learner put it into an appropriate perspective or extract the appropriate subject matter.

In short, the fact that a trainer uses a good deal of media in his or her instruction fails to guarantee effectiveness. The media must be carefully selected or designed to serve the purpose of training as stated in the instructional objectives.

2.3 Deductive approach.

This approach has to do with assisting the learner to draw specific inferences from given generalizations. It offers something more than a straightforward expository approach which simply puts information forth for the learner's consumption. In using the deductive approach, the trainer attempts to draw the learner into active application of a general rule or procedure to specific cases.

So, for instance, the trainer of Social Security claims authorizers may give the general rule that evidence of at least 40 quarters of earnings covered by Social Security is required for the minimum benefit at retirement. The learner may then be given hypothetical cases in which he or she must establish whether each case qualifies for minimum benefits.

2.4 Inductive approach

In this approach the learner is exposed to a number of specific cases or situations from which he or she is to draw a generalization. This normally requires much more time and effort than the deductive approach and is only practical when it is important for the learner to be committed intellectually and emotionally to the generalization by forming it through his or her own reasoning processes.

For example, a trainer of supervisors may wish to gain learner commitment to the principle that dealing directly with an employee's consistently poor performance is generally more effective than ignoring it. He or she may therefore design or compile a set of case studies which shows the results of different supervisory approaches with the intention that the learner will form the generalization. That generalization, along with other learner insights, may then be sharpened through group discussion. The point here is that while putting the learner through a set of case studies is much more time consuming than simply stating the generalization for the learner, the ultimate change in the learner's behavior is apt to be far more profound and lasting. Thus, in a case like this, the inductive approach is not only justified but preferred.

2.5 Part to whole approach.

This approach is specifically for motor skill learning. It consists of guiding the learner step-by-step through successive parts of a skill, such as tuning an engine or installing an appliance. Emphasis is on achieving mastery on each part before integrating all the parts into a complete performance. The challenge to the instructor here is to be able to divide the performance into logical and convenient parts for instructional purposes so that the learner is able to master each part with relative ease.

2.6 Whole to part approach.

There are occasions when the trainer may wish to have the learner practice the integrated skill before concentrating on mastering individual components. Sports provide good examples of this. The advantage of practicing the integrated skill first is that it allows the learner to practice his or her component skills in an integrated context as well as separately. The separate performance of the component skill sharpens that one component while the performance of the whole skill brings the component into efficient coordination with the other components. Thus, the soccer novice may learn first to scrimmage, then begin to concentrate on ball-handling skills.

2.7 Modeling.

By modeling, more is meant than mere demonstration of a performance. Modeling implies conveying to the learner a style or attitude. A trainer may demonstrate how to install a heating system or an elevator or how to disassemble a weapon, but he or she would model interviewing or counseling or public speaking. Modeling can be a powerful instructional method. It is most appropriate for teaching those dimensions of performance which are difficult to convey in purely rational terms. Qualities of human interaction such as deference, gentle firmness or warmth can be modeled far more effectively than they can be described.

3. EVOKE LEARNING.

3.1 Memorization.

Memorization has largely fallen into disfavor in public education over the past two generations, primarily because educators came to realize that memorized answers and formulas were not sufficient for coping successfully in modern society. Their thinking was basically sound, but it has created successive generations of adults who have little experience with memorization. This means that often neither trainers nor their learners think of using it, even when it can serve an instructional purpose.

Memorization serves to focus the learner very deliberately upon a given fact or body of information. Thus, a file clerk may memorize the rule—"always record on the inventory sheet the identification number of a claims folder when removing it from the file." Or a brakeman may memorize the rule—"always check for clearance before stepping out from between cars."

Memorization should be reserved for actions which are of crucial importance in job performance. Failure to record a pulled file could frustrate attempts to locate a claim quickly by breaking the audit chain. Several unregistered file removals can eventually lead to serious delays and costly search activity in the claims record system. The brakeman's failure to look before stepping out from between cars can lead to a serious and perhaps fatal accident. His or her internalization of the rule is of crucial importance, to say the least.

Memorization does not guarantee proper performance. The trainer should not rely solely upon this learning device but should use it in combination with demonstration, practice and feedback, as appropriate. Consequently, the trainer of the brakeman should provide the learner opportunities to practice the safety rules he or she has memorized in as authentic a work setting as possible.

As for the learner's ability to memorize, the trainer should provide whatever instructional support is necessary, such as displaying and reviewing the information repeatedly and asking the learner to recall it periodically. Usually, repeated exposure and recitation is sufficient, though the trainer may wish to take more trouble and guide the learner in forming meaningful associations between what is to be memorized and what the learner already knows.

3.2 Concept formation.

An individual shows that he or she has learned a concept when he or she can explain or demonstrate the meaning of some particular class of objects, events or relations. Technical training in particular introduces the learner to many new concepts. Take for example the training of real estate appraisers who must master dozens of concepts concerned with property and value. The following list of concepts is merely suggestive:
- Real property.
- Personal property.
- Value in use.
- Value in exchange.
- Preliminary survey.
- Encroachment.
- Infiltration.
- Site valuation.
- Plottage.
- Depth table.
- Corner influence.

- Easement.
- Effective gross income.
- Capitalization.
- Land residual.
- Leasehold value.

The most effective way to teach concepts is through a combination of definition, example and comparison and contrast. For example, let's consider the first two concepts from the above list.

Definition

1. Real property: this refers to the ownership of physical real estate (physical land and appurtenances).

2. Personal property: this refers generally to movable items not permanently affixed to and part of the real estate.

Example

1. Real property: house, fence, bridge, tree, natural resources, plumbing, electricity, heating, built-in cabinets.

2. Personal property: furniture, office equipment, livestock, stocks and bonds, jewelry, automobile.

Comparison and contrast

The distinction between personal property and real property is an important one for the appraiser, for if a fixture were personal property, it would not go with the real estate and its contribution to the value of the real property could not be considered. But if the fixture were real property, its value could be considered. For example, if a portable safe were simply set in a corner on a table, it would constitute personal property. However, if it were installed in a wall, it would become part of the real property. Similarly, if shelving were left free-standing it would be personal property; if it were attached to a wall, it would generally be regarded as part of the real property.

Now, our separate treatment in this chapter of memorization and concept formation are mere conveniences. Actually, the learner will exercise some memorization of the terms that represent the concepts. The key distinction here is that the learner is not simply storing information. Rather, he or she is forming new concepts to be used to give meaning to particular classes of objects, events or relationships. To contrast the two, concepts equate to real property and personal property, while information equates to the fact that real property and personal property are taxed at different rates in most states.

3.3. Rule learning.

Concepts serve largely as building blocks for carrying out the vast number of activities entailed in a job. Most of that activity can be described as rule-using or procedural. Therefore, most of the trainer's time will go into teaching procedures—the ways of accomplishing job tasks. The trainer should break each procedure down into its subcomponents and make sure the learner knows all necessary concepts and understands each subordinate activity.

For example, the real estate appraiser must learn to estimate the gross income of a property as part of the valuation process. In order to do this, he or she must not only understand the concept of gross income but must also know how to do the following:

a. Acquire pertinent facts about the property, its environs and peculiarities.

b. Determine how current economic, social and political trends are affecting the property or are likely to affect it.

c. Identify rentals earned by similar properties.

d. Estimate the amount which tenants, present and prospective, can afford to pay.

The more precise the trainer is in presenting the rules and procedures, the greater the likelihood that the learner will comprehend it clearly. He or she can do this by clearly delineating each of the subordinate activities. Of course, in addition to precise presentation, the learner will need practice in actually performing the procedure. There is no adequate substitute for practice.

3.4 Attitude development.

Attitude was described in Chapter 2 as involving beliefs, assumptions, perceptions, feelings or preferences toward an internal or external stimulus. It cannot be conveyed to the learner as directly as information or concepts and procedures. Modeling was described earlier in this chapter as perhaps the most effective method for conveying attitude. However it is transmitted, the learner should be encouraged to demonstrate the attitude. As with learning rules, practice is essential.

In claims processing, for example, the trainer wishes to develop a belief on the part of the learner that a claim is not processed until all required information is supplied. This attitude is an important one since one of the biggest problems claims units face is the volume of cases requiring partial rework due to incomplete initial processing. In order to establish and reinforce this belief, the trainer needs to place the learner in a controlled situation in which he or she must exert extra effort to acquire the information needed to complete the case. The trainer guides the learner as necessary so that he or she experiences the success of completing a difficult case. The experience, repeated at intervals, should prepare the learner to stay with challenging cases until their completion on the actual job.

4. PROVIDE FEEDBACK.

4.1 Verbal feedback.

Verbal feedback to the learner regarding his or her performance can be given orally or in writing. For example, if the learner has just demonstrated how to persuade through a prepared speech, it may be most effective to provide oral feedback right on the spot, focusing first on the good points, then on the aspects that need improvement. It is also good to follow up this immediate oral feedback with more detailed written comment which can be more readily studied and retained for future application.

4.2 Performance feedback.

There are a number of ways other than verbal to provide the learner with accurate feedback. One involves providing the learner with sufficiently clear and detailed criteria so that he or she can assess his or her own work. For example, the learner works a case, then receives a handout which describes each essential action which should have been taken. By matching his or her responses with the criteria given in the handout, the learner can catch mistakes and perhaps discover the source of errors or omissions.

Another method of providing feedback on performance is through the use of audio or video tape, particularly where personal interaction skills are involved. Playback can be supplemented by either instructor comments or a criterion sheet so that the learner has as much as possible at hand to help him or her improve or maintain performance.

A third and often more challenging way is to design feedback into the performance itself. Biofeedback is a good example of this with the learner able to monitor the effects of his or her performance constantly. Of course, the narrower the tolerances for mistakes, the more crucial feedback becomes. Thus, air traffic controllers must obtain precise, immediate and frequent feedback on their practice of skills which are necessary for maintaining the safety of hundreds of people at a given moment. Some of the criteria for adequate performance can be computer programmed, so that the learner's performance at a terminal automatically sets off predetermined feedback when performance fails to meet criteria.

4.3 Reinforcement.

In behavioral psychology, to reinforce means to increase the likelihood that a particular behavior will be repeated. The trainer can do just that by providing feedback to the learner. From behavioral psychology we learn that positive feedback makes the best reinforcer. Therefore, the trainer should make a point of responding to "appropriate" or "good" or "desired" performance as opposed to only providing corrective feedback for inadequate performance.

A reinforcer is any stimulus that tends to increase desired behavior. For one learner, just learning that his or her performance met criteria might be reinforcing. Indeed, test scores can be powerful reinforcers. For another learner, some expression of personal satisfaction on the part of the trainer might be an effective reinforcer. For a third learner, peer recognition of good performance might be most reinforcing. To design the most effective reinforcers for learners, the trainer must understand what essentially motivates them within the instructional setting.

5. TEST PERFORMANCE.

5.1 Actual performance.

There is no better way to assure that the learner can perform a task than by testing him or her on that task repeatedly. For example, a cartographer may be given actual assignments in map construction or map modification. Since his or her work can be monitored and evaluated before it is sent on, there is little risk of loss involved. Actual performance is an appropriate and preferable means of testing for this particular learned performance, so long as the criteria for acceptable performance have been clearly established.

Moreover, the trainer should not wait to test at the end of instruction but should test as frequently as possible as a means of diagnosing learner progress and providing feedback to the learner. This means that information, concepts and procedures should be tested regularly at a reasonable cost in time, effort and resources. For example, in order to enter data into a word processor, the operator must first be able to use the alpha-numeric keys with some proficiency and must be able to identify each action key. The trainer can test the learner's ability to perform each of these sub-skills right on the word processor.

5.2 Simulation.

More often than not, the trainer will be prohibited from testing the learner on actual job task performance. It may be too expensive, too disruptive or risky because of the sensitive or inherently dangerous nature of the work. But there are many ways of simulating real environments. The military are the past-masters of simulation with flight trainers, firing ranges, survival courses and field maneuvers.

It is perhaps the trainer's greatest challenge to design and construct simulations that represent real performance situations with high fidelity. Success lies in accomplishing a simulation so effective that a learner's performance on the simulation is a virtually certain predictor of performance in actual situations. Frequently, the trainer will require the assistance of technical specialists in designing and constructing the simulation, but he or she must be the judge of what criteria the simulation must meet in order to sufficiently prepare the learner.

5.3 Substitution

In Chapter 3, substitution was described as the least effective means of testing performance. Yet, it is frequently the only reasonable means of assessment. Consider a trainer who has been given one hour to convey to medical secretaries several changes in report and documentation requirements for patient care administrative processing. He or she may be able to devise only a quick test which asks the learner to match a given report or document with several types of administrative actions.

This test does not indicate whether the medical secretaries will be able to initiate the appropriate forms and documents back on the job or whether they will be able to complete accurately the forms once they initiate them. It only shows whether they are able immediately following instruction to match the right form or document (when provided) with a given administrative action. But it is, nevertheless, a means of discovering whether some critical learning has taken place.

The trainer may have to compromise frequently when it comes to providing opportunities for the learner to practice actual performance and for the trainer to test actual performance. The evaluator needs to be aware of the trainer's constraints so that he or she may judge the reasonableness of the trainer's methods and recommend ways of overcoming those constraints where feasible.

6. FOLLOW-THROUGH.

6.1 Overlearning.
Experience tells us that knowledge and skill deteriorate from lack of use. This fact should play a prominent part in the design of training for people who cannot routinely apply certain learned knowledge and skills in the normal course of their work.

It is convenient for us to think of training as having a well-defined end point, for closed-ended training greatly facilitates the scheduling of people, places and materials. But where necessary, we should provide opportunities for the learner to recapture or resharpen his or her knowledge or skill. This type of training is often called "refresher" training.

However, there is something more we can do to inhibit the deterioration of learning. We can facilitate "overlearning." Overlearning means practicing a skill or applying knowledge over and over again, well beyond the point where performance criteria are first met. Athletes are trained this way. They practice fundamentals routinely despite the fact that they may have already rendered consistently superior performance.

Skills that are overlearned can deteriorate, but at a dramatically reduced rate from what it would otherwise be. People who took piano lessons as children will typically find that after a few moments of groping at a keyboard, they can still play the scales with proper finger positioning or perhaps play at least a fragment of a piece they had once learned. The same holds true for typing or swimming or skipping rope.

Overlearning can be applied to any variety of performances. Consider its use, for example, in the training of lifeguards.

They may have few opportunities to use their life-saving skills, but when these skills are called upon, they must be automatic and exact. Training in interpersonal communications could also profit from overlearning, so that the trained individual is not hesitant to use interpersonal communicatin skills and can rely on responses which have been tried and tested several times—second nature rather than awkward and new.

6.2 Certification.
When a course or training program is designed and conducted in such a way that learners are able to demonstrate a clear set of acquired skills and knowledge, then it is proper and useful to certify in some public way that an individual now possesses those skills and knowledge. In fact, the learner's performance capabilities should be detailed as completely as possible within reasonable limits. A brief

list of major skills or topics mastered could easily be displayed along with a course title on a paper certificate. This suggestion may seem somewhat extraordinary, but present practice of merely stating the name of the course is only a matter of convention. Ultimately, a more detailed certificate can assist both the individual and an employer or prospective employer by clarifying what the person can really do as a result of his or her training.

Trainers frequently distribute certificates of attendance or completion. These certificates do not carry much currency as compared with certificates of achievement or performance because the former in no way certify that any meaningful learning has taken place. Of course, for some instructional formats which do not call for the teaching and testing of specific skills or knowledge, such certificates are at least accurate symbols of the learner's activity.

6.3 Prescription.

In some cases, certification is not possible or advisable. Consider cases where the learner has failed to meet minimal criteria in his or her performance. Here some sort of prescription is called for—recycling the learner through all or parts of the same instruction, providing the learner with alternate means of studying and then testing again or recommending that the learner be placed in a more appropriate job or training program.

Even in cases where the learner can be certified, the trainer may be able to make useful recommendations to the individual or the organization. The learner may still need to work on a particular skill or may need close supervision at some of his or her job tasks at first. Some learners may give evidence of unusual technical or leadership ability. The organization may find it useful to acknowledge and respond to this ability quickly and should be informed of it. In brief, the trainer has the opportunity to observe closely the individual's ability to learn and to perform. Therefore, he or she should be encouraged to prescribe post training options for the learner where they are useful and realistic.

Applying the Model

Given the Model of Instruction for Training, how can the evaluator use it to assess the trainer's instructional strategies? Remembering that the MIT is a guide, not a prescription for strategies, the evaluator can first look for evidence that the trainer has considered each of the six basic principles. Then he or she can check to determine whether they appear adequate for the purpose of training and making recommendations for changes and additions where appropriate. The MIT Review Guide provides a format for this purpose.

MIT Review Guide

Course/program under review:
Objective(s) or unit of coverage:

Principle/method used

	Method is consistent with objective(s)	Method is effective	Method needs modification	Recommended method	Comments*
1. Prepare the learner					
___ 1.1 Dramatize purpose and importance of subject matter.					
___ 1.2 Review previous learning.					
___ 1.3 Provide framework for understanding.					
___ 1.4 Trigger curiosity.					
2. Present stimuli.					
___ 2.1 Verbal communication.					
___ 2.2 Mediated communication.					
___ 2.3 Deductive approach.					
___ 2.4 Inductive approach.					
___ 2.5 Part to whole approach.					
___ 2.6 Whole to part approach.					
___ 2.7 Modeling.					
3. Evoke learning.					
___ 3.1 Memorization.					
___ 3.2 Concept formation.					
___ 3.3 Rule learning.					
___ 3.4 Attitude development.					
4. Provide feedback.					
___ 4.1 Verbal feedback.					
___ 4.2 Performance feedback.					
___ 4.3 Reinforcement.					
5. Test performance.					
___ 5.1 Actual performance.					
___ 5.2 Simulation.					
___ 5.3 Substitution.					
6. Follow-through.					
___ 6.1 Overlearning.					
___ 6.2 Certification.					
___ 6.3 Prescription.					

*The evaluator can assist the trainer by providing a detailed description of his or her analysis and recommendations for change.

Actual Training Events

Up to this point, we have scrutinized the planning that goes into instruction—the objectives, the tests and the instructional strategies. But we have yet to address the instruction itself—the actual events of training. In training, as in many undertakings, the best laid plans often go awry. It is important for the evaluator to establish an accurate account of what actually transpired in the training sessions in order to know (1) whether the instructional strategy was effectively carried out; and (2) whether that strategy turned out to be appropriate for the learner and the actual setting.

Potential Problems

There are any number of things that can interfere with actual instruction. The three most common are described here:

1. *Lack of time.* It is easy to underestimate the amount of time needed for instruction. Participants frequently have questions or comments that precipitate departures from the instructional outline or lesson plan. In other cases, participants require more time than expected to complete assignments or master the instructional objectives.

2. *Learners not ready for level of planned instruction.* Time can be a problem even when the participants are equipped with the necessary prerequisite skills and experience. It is much more of a problem when they are not so equipped. A course may be designed with the presumption that the learner understands algebraic concepts. If he or she does not, that lack of knowledge may be an insuperable barrier to achieving the performance objectives.

3. *Instructor not ready to instruct.* There is nothing more embarrassing and frustrating both for instructor and for learner than an instructor who is not qualified or adequately prepared to give the instruction assigned to him or her. The most competently designed instructional program may fall woefully short of achieving its objectives if the trainer is not adequately prepared to carry it out effectively.

There are other potential interferences with the instructional plan—equipment failure, poor physical plant conditions, changes in work and class schedules, etc. To the degree the evaluator can identify these interferences and the effects they have on actual instruction, he or she will be able to judge (1) whether the instructional strategy was implemented in fact (for all practical purposes); and (2) whether that strategy was indeed appropriate for the learner and the instructional setting.

The following format is offered as an aid to the evaluator in recording observations of instructional events. It builds upon the six principles of instructional strategy and the common interferences to implementing strategy, both described above, as well as upon expectations about the learner and the instructional support system.

Instructional Observation Checklist

Instructor	Yes	No	Comments
1. Instructor's remarks and activities were well organized.			
2. Instructor's knowledge of subject matter was sufficient for purposes of training.			
3. Element of time was well-managed.			
4. Strategy was modified to meet the needs of the learner.			
5. Strategy was modified to meet unanticipated problems (time, material, equipment, environment).			
6. Learners were adequately prepared by instructor for stimuli.			
7. Stimuli were presented effectively.			
8. Appropriate learning strategies were used.			
9. Useful feedback was provided to the learner.			
10. Performance was effectively tested.			
11. Test results were followed up by the instructor.			

Learners

	Yes	No	Comments
12. Learning needs and abilities were accurately anticipated in the planned instruction.			
13. Learners appeared prepared for the instruction, mentally, physically and attitudinally.			
14. Learners responded positively to the instructor's direction.			

Instructional Support System

	Yes	No	Comments
15. Adequate space was allocated for instructional activities.			
16. Sufficient instructional material was available.			
17. Sufficient and operable equipment was available.			
18. Lighting, heating and ventilation were adequate.			
19. Instructional area was free from outside disturbances.			
20. Chairs, tables and other furnishings were appropriately arranged to meet instructional needs.			

Summary

Having established the objectives for the learner with criteria for acceptable performance and having determined how to test performance, the trainer's next immediate challenges are to devise an instructional strategy that will effectively bring the learner to criteria and then, with equal effectiveness, carry out that strategy through the actual instructional events. The evaluator can provide the trainer with a model for developing instructional strategies as well as using the model as a guide for assessing the trainer's strategies. He or she can also provide the trainer with useful feedback on his or her effectiveness in implementing strategies in the actual events of instruction.

Review of Progress

Evaluator Task #3: Assess the appropriateness and adequacy of instructional strategies, both as planned and as carried out in the actual events of instruction.

Enabling Skills:

• Ability to apply a comprehensive model of instructional strategy to a given instructional plan.

• Ability to assess the trainer's effectiveness in implementing his or her instructional strategy.

Chapter 5

They Loved It— But Will They Use It?

We have dealt thus far with all the aspects of instructional planning and implementation: planning with performance objectives, designing criterion-referenced tests, developing instructional strategies and implementing those strategies through the actual events of training. Now we turn to the transfer of learning from training to actual performance.

Follow-up assessment is an uncommon practice in many organizations. Yet it is not uncommon for managers to complain that many of their employees never reach an adequate level of performance on the job. Assessment of the transfer of learning from training to actual performance is the exception rather than the rule because it is not firmly established as a necessary component of organizational and human resource development.

But it can be. It takes an evaluator with the ability to perform follow-up assessment and a decision maker who is convinced that it is important to know whether training has the impact it is assumed to have on human performance.

As a result of this chapter, the reader should be able to match the right follow-up assessment methods with different types of performance and select or design checklists for use in the assessment process. The major assessment methods or approaches are the following:

- Direct observation.
- Third-party observation.
- Assessment centers.
- Study of work results.
- Learner self-reporting.

Each approach will be treated separately, and each is recommended for differing needs or purposes. A disproportionate amount of detail is provided for the last method treated, the learner self-reporting approach, primarily because learner self-reporting has been poorly done in the main and therefore has lost much of its credibility. Yet it remains a viable, and in some cases, necessary option for the training evaluator.

Direct Observation

One way to assess whether learning has been transferred to the actual performance situation is by observing the learner some time after training in the performance situation. Not all tasks can be observed easily without interfering, but many can. Safety procedures for shops and assembly lines can be observed unobtrusively as can many manipulative tasks.

The evaluator may wish to bring a set of notes on criteria for acceptable level of performance to help him or her in his or her obser-

---

Traffic Control Observation Checklist

Controller Observed: Date:

Evaluator: Location:

Traffic Complexity: ☐ Routine   ☐ Occasionally Difficult   ☐ Very Difficult

Performance Criteria:	Satisfactory Performance	Not Observed	Unsatisfactory Performance	Comments
1. Obtained all facts concerning the control situation.				
2. Determined the requirements of aircraft.				
3. Issued only necessary restrictions.				
4. Utilized correct vector procedures.				
5. Correctly evaluated factors affecting safety of aircraft.				
6. Corrected evaluated factors affecting traffic flow.				
7. Informed appropriate personnel of existing significant situations.				
8. Corrected for unnecessary separation.				
9. Corrected for altitude, heading or speed changes.				
10. Initiated procedures in a timely and orderly manner.				

vation. These notes will help the evaluator keep his or her attention centered upon performance in the midst of distracting activities. For example, the following checklist might be used by an evaluator to assess task performance of a new air traffic controller. The task is *traffic management control* with the learning objective being *the ability to demonstrate appropriate traffic control practices as required to maintain an efficient flow of traffic.* Each of the performance criteria which together define the acceptable level of performance are accounted for in the checklist.

The value in such a follow-up to training is that it identifies specific areas in which the trained performer may need additional instruction or coaching, and it identifies those portions of instruction which require review for possible alteration. If, for example, several recent air traffic controller graduates were found lacking in the sub-skill of using correct vector procedures, then that portion of training should be analyzed for possible redesign or reinforcement.

Third-Party Observation

Third-party assessment requires highly reliable instruments or highly reliable observers but it can be informative and practical. It consists of eliciting responses from people who interact regularly with the trained performer and who are aware of the quality of the performance or the results of the performance. Third-party observation is particularly useful for performance that cannot be directly observed by the trainer.

Consider a claims representative whose job it is to counsel individuals regarding their eligibility for Social Security, Medicaid or disability compensation and to initiate the claims process with the claimant. You may recall from Chapter 2 a description of a performance test in which serveral criteria were given for demonstrating client interviewing skills. Just as those criteria were suggested as an aid for observing performance in a simulated interview, they may be used by the supervisor who is often present in the office when the claims representative is interacting with a client. These criteria are shown below in a checklist for supervisors.

These performance criteria may serve at the same time as a means for rating work performance and as a means for diagnosing the need for refresher training or on-the-job coaching by the supervisor.

Client Interview Checklist

Criteria for Interviewing	Not Observed	Satisfactory	Exemplary	Unsatisfactory	Comments
1. The client is set at ease.					
2. Questions are posed in a non-threatening way.					
3. Probing is included where necessary.					
4. All essential information is elicited.					
5. All essential information is fully and accurately recorded.					
6. The interviewer maintains a professional demeanor.					
7. Correct procedural information is given to the client in a manner the client can understand.					

Assessment Centers

To extend our example of the claims representative, suppose client interviews are conducted in privacy. Then the supervisor is limited in his or her assessment of the interviewer's performance. This is where the assessment center may be most effective. Basically, the assessment center method involves putting the individual through a set of simulated problems, tasks or job situations which test the individual's ability to perform effectively. It can be used prior to instruction as a means for determining training needs or for estimating the potential an individual possesses for acquiring certain performance skills. It can also be used sometime after the trained individual has begun performing on the job.

If the individual has been applying the skills or knowledge learned through instruction, there should be evidence of it in the assessment center performance tests. Just as the trainer may use role playing to test the individual's ability to interview a client during training, so may he or she present the individual with similar role playing situations in the follow-up assessment. Presumably, if the individual has been applying the appropriate skills, he or she should perform at least as well and probably better than at the conclusion of training. If the follow-up assessment shows a deterioration of skills, the trainer or evaluator can presume that those skills have not been used much on the job.

Assessment centers require an explicit expenditure in human and material resources. Therefore they are less economical than direct observation or third-party observation. Their virture lies in their potential for focusing with greater precision on particular performance skills which are difficult to observe in the normal performance setting.

Study of Work Results

Unlike the tasks described above, there are many complex performances which are not readily observable, either in the natural performance setting or in a simulated environment. For example, analysts of all types—systems analysts, program analysts, management analysts, budget analysts, etc.—tend to work on projects or problems in stages over long periods of time. Much of their work is mental and therefore not accessible to observation. And many of their activities demand unique responses which fulfill the unique requirements of the project or problem they may face, thus defying any convenient universal criteria for actual performance.

For these kinds of performance, we may turn to a study of work results for a means to assess whether learning has been transferred to the job. For example, an analyst's report on his or her review of a program could be assessed against the criteria for work results shown below. These criteria can be both the minimal criteria for acceptable training performance as well as the essential elements of program analysis reporting as it is taught.

Essential Elements of Program Analysis Reporting

1. The problem is defined.
2. Evaluation criteria are described.
3. Client groups are specified.
4. Alternatives are identified for solving the problem or satisfying the objective.
5. Costs are estimated for each alternative.
6. Probable effectiveness of each alternative is determined.
7. Findings are displayed in appropriate formats.
8. Analysis is reviewed before distribution.
9. A clear, concise summary accompanies the report.
10. Limitations and assumptions of the study are described.
11. Writing is free of jargon and adheres to normal standards of composition.
12. Report is tailored to the needs of the client groups.

The evaluator's application of this list of essential elements or criteria to a new analyst's report would reveal to the evaluator those components of learning which were not transferred successfully by the learner from the training to the job. And, of course, had the learner's performance not been assessed during or immediately following training, the follow-up assessment would signal the possibility that the learner never did adequately master the learning objectives.

In this case, the evaluator may learn from studying the work results (reports) that analysts are not carefully identifying the clients who need the report and thus are not always focusing on the appropriate problem for analysis. The evaluator may discover upon further inquiry that analysts are not working with their managers in identifying the decision makers who really need the analysis results and thus are failing to identify problems or objectives which are central to those decision makers' concerns. These discoveries may lead to a modification of training to include instruction on working with managers to better define clients and problems.

Work results come in many forms that can be analyzed for learning transfer. If machinists are trained in a new method for reducing waste in their processing of rolling stock, then systematic inspection of waste disposal areas should reveal whether the machinists have successfully transfered the method to the work place. If brakemen are given refresher training on safety procedures in equipment handling due to an alarming rate of accidents, then accidents incurred by brakemen from handling equipment should decline noticeably. And if real estate agents are trained to screen the prospective buyer for financial capacity, the broker should see few instances of buyers being denied mortgage loans when lenders have money for mortgages.

Learner Self-Reporting

Depending upon the learner's own testimony for an assessment of learning seems risky. After all, the learner is less likely to be objective about his or her performance than is an observer. However, there are many circumstances in which little or no observation of actual performance is feasible. Moreover, there is a way to bring a reasonable measure of objectivity to self-reporting and to use it as a means for assessing the transfer of learning to the job.

The most effective way to generate accurate and practical self-reporting on learning transfer is by making the learner a partner in the formulation of an action plan which he or she carries back to the job and implements to the extent he or she can. This approach has been taught as a "self-change agenda technique" by James N. Mosel of George Washington University and has been incorporated into a more fully developed system at the U.S. Office of Personnel Management. Called the Participant Action Plan Approach (PAPA), this sytem serves explicitly as a means for assessing the degree to which the individual has been able to put into practice what he or she has gained from instruction in the way of insights, methods or solutions to problems. (U.S. Office of Personnel Management, *A Guide to the Participant Action Plan Approach.* OPM: Washington, D.C. 1979.)

PAPA's Five Basic Steps

In general, PAPA requires that participants develop action plans at the end of training—lists of behaviors they want to try out when they return to their jobs. The plans should be based in some way on the training just experienced. After some time has elapsed, the participants are contacted to see what changes they have actually implemented. This process is carried out in the following five steps.

Step 1: Planning for PAPA. In this step, the evaluator determines the specific activities needed in this application, considering the available resources and the needs of the organization. He or she then assigns and schedules the tasks necessary to carry out the approach, e.g., preparing handouts, scheduling appearances at the training session, scheudling follow-up interviews, and preparing an evaluation report.

Step 2: In-Course Activities. This step consist of two stages. At the beginning of the training, learners are introduced to the idea of an action plan and asked to consider throughout the course what they might want to do differently on their jobs as a result of training. Then, at the end of instruction, they are asked to write an action plan—a list of new, training-related activities which they plan to try when they return to the job.

A portion of such an action plan might look like this:

I plan to:

    1. Involve my employees in developing performance criteria for job performance.

    2. Review performance with each employee informally at least quarterly.

Step 3: Follow-up Activities. At a prearranged time after training, usually several months later, learners are interviewed or contacted by questionnaire. They are asked which of their planned activities they have been able to achieve up to that time as well as what other new activities they have attempted as a result of having attended training. They are also asked what effects their new behaviors have had on their work environment, and what problems, if any, they have encountered in trying these new behaviors.

Step 4: Analysis and Conclusions. In this step, the data collected during the follow-up are sorted, categorized and displayed in order to show the extent and type of change. The information can be displayed in the form of descriptions of behavioral change; it can be summarized numerically, e.g., how many of the learners instituted performance standards for their employees; or it can be reported using a combination of narrative and numbers.

Step 5: Report. The findings from the analysis and the conclusions and recommendations regarding the training can be reported through a written document or through a management presentation, whatever form best meets the needs of the organization.

Alternate Ways of Implementing PAPA

Aside from the choice of whether to contact the learner through live interview, phone interview or questionnaire, the evaluator has some additional options in using PAPA. He or she may choose to contact a sample of participants rather than the entire group; he or she may seek corroborating information on changed behavior from supervisors or peers who work with the learner; and he or she may supplement his or her questions regarding the learner's planned activities with questions about the learner's assessment of the training.

Application of PAPA to An Emergency Management Course

The author used PAPA to evaluate the impact of a course on emergency management given to a group of eleven emergency management professionals. These individuals had come together for training from five states in the mid-Atlantic region. The nature of the emergency manager's work calls for considerable autonomy, and the person he or she normally reports to (mayor, city manager, county executive) interacts very little with him or her. Most of the work involves planning and coordinating, but perhaps the most universal characteristic of the job is that each emergency manager is faced with different problems, different inherent assets and liabilities in his or her jurisdiction, and different political environments.

This combination of characteristics amounted to a group which had some generic tasks and problems in common but which had also a wide assortment of specific concerns most pressing to each individual. As for deciding upon an assessment strategy for the instruction, direct observation was out of the question due to the nature of the work and the dispersed geographical locations of the work sites; third-party observation was no better a solution due to the limited contact between the learner and his or her supervisor; and work results were highly dependent upon the type of jurisdiction in which the learner served. Therefore, learner self-assessment was chosen as the most appropriate means for checking on transfer of learning. What follows is a brief reconstruction of the evaluation.

Preparing the Participants

On the first morning of the instructional session, the evaluator was introduced. He explained to the course participants that they would be asked to develop action items or objectives which they would like to carry out back on their jobs. These action items would be related either to the prescribed subject matter of the course or they could come from something the instructional activity precipitated, including spin-offs from interaction with other participants over job-related concerns.

The evaluator also explained that each participant would be called in about two months to find out whether he or she had been able to implement those activities. The participants were given handouts 1 and 2 (end of chapter) with some illustrations of the kinds of action items or activities which might be appropriate for this course session.

The evaluator also explained during this initial session that participants would be given some time each morning to review the course activities of the preceding day and to formulate some ideas for action items. During those subsequent mornings, the evaluator reminded the participants of the action planning format and initiated a 10-15 minute period for idea generation (some discussion was held between individuals, but this was largely a private activity).

Action Planning Session

At the completion of course instruction, the evaluator directed the participants to review their action item ideas and to select those items they wished to develop into formal action items. Approximately 20 minutes were devoted to this activity.

The evaluator then directed the participants to share their action plans with one other class member and to exchange critiques providing each other with feedback—did they understand each other's items, and could they offer suggestions for implementing those items? Approximately 20 additional minutes were spent on this exchange.

Finally, the evaluator asked participants to write their action items in duplicate form (see handout 3 at end of chapter). He collected a copy of each form, reminding the participants that he would be calling by phone in approximately eight weeks to ask whether each had been able to implement plans.

Follow-up

Six weeks after the course's completion date, the evaluator sent out a letter which reminded participants of the action planning and the evaluation follow-up. They were told in the letter that they would be called for a phone interview, and were told the date and time. Calls were placed during the eighth week to arrange those interviews, and the actual phone interviews were conducted during the ninth and tenth weeks. An interview guide was used to record the information.

Results of Interviews

All but three people were successfully interviewed during the follow-up. Of the three not successfully interviewed, one simply indicated she did not have time for the follow-up (this individual had expressed a great deal of personal frustration during the course); a second person indicated his action plan was superfluous since he had no time to carry it out; and a third person was on extended vacation during the interview period. Thus, with the knowledge that two people found extremely little from the course to apply on the job, the following analysis centers on the data generated by the eight people who were successfully interviewed.

1. Individual responses. The responses of each person interviewed were transferred from the original interview form to a matrix form which identified action items, behavior, outcomes and problems. These matrices show just what the participant had done with respect to each action item, what resulted from his or her actions and what problems were encountered, if any.

These matrices amounted to a great deal of specific information, and while much of it was abstracted on to a simpler form (planned behaviors) displayed below, the matrices yield a sufficiently detailed picture to give the course instructor or manager a full grasp of the course's impact.

a. Participant A appears to have achieved two noteworthy undertakings: he has successfully prompted two of his staff members to register for Phase II, and he had begun work on mediated information packages for the public on disaster signals and signs.

b. Participant B has succeeded in giving a city government a more detailed emergency plan than it possessed heretofore; and she was able to use "legitimizers" to obtain a more effective emergency transportation service for the community.

c. Participant C has created a strategy for cultivating key local figures whose support is needed for successful crisis relocation planning; she has also convinced her administration of the need for additional staff planners.

d. Participant D was able to gain specific support for the implementation of a nuclear civil protection plan; he was also able to develop detailed work plans for himself and his staff which will serve as a three-year plan for his operation.

e. Participant E has had difficulty implementing her objectives but claims she has better insight into her organization's budget process and a stronger appreciation for the role of legitimizers in the social process.

f. Participant F has discovered that she can reach influential organization and community figures to inform them of the county's civil defense program. She is finding these people receptive and willing to talk.

g. Participant G appears to have used very little of what she learned, at least in any practical way which she could describe in terms of behavior and outcomes.

h. Participant H has been able to use planning and budgeting concepts from the course in developing his Radiological Emergency Plan and in performing a cost analysis of the state's radiological maintenance and calibration shop.

2. Evaluator Observations about Actions Taken. A few readily observable characteristics can be described on the basis of the interview data:

a. Most of the participants were able to implement at least one and usually two action items of some consequence in their organizations.

b. The nature of the action plans and actual behaviors varied widely among individual participants.
c. With a few exceptions, the participants experienced few problems in implementing their plans.

3. Participants as a Group. In reviewing the group's success in carrying out, at least to some degree, the action items they had generated in class, we can see that almost all the action items were implemented (see Figure 1). This suggests that participants took a pragmatic approach to planning their post-course activities and that they took seriously their responsibilities for attempting to carry them out. It also suggests that the course was capable of prompting useful follow-up activities on the part of the participants who for the most part chose action items related to the course content.

Figure 1
Group Success in
Implementing Planned Behaviors

Planned Behaviors	Number of Participants Mentioning Planned Behaviors	Number Actually Implemented
Meet with budget analyst to discuss budget and increase chance of its approval.	1	1
Perform cost analysis of state radiological maintenance and calibration shop for inclusion in FY'82 budget request.	1	1
Discuss this course at meeting with superior or staff.	2	2
Identify legitimizers to overcome assistance to program.	2	2
Seek community support for budget.	3	1
Seek support within agency for program.	1	1
Complete basic emergency plan with assistance from government agencies and the community legitimizers.	1	1
Justify need for additional staff	1	1
Develop overall plan for work, e.g., objectives, PERT.	2	2
Provide input on headquarters proposal.	1	0
Review records of successful department efforts.	1	0
Prepare a budget.	1	1
Devise "mail-stuffer" on civil defense.	1	1
Total	18	14

4. Participant Critique of Training. It is interesting to note that comments about the training varied to the extreme (see Figure 2). Twenty comments were offered by the eight interviewed participants and in only two instances did more than one person make comments almost identical to another person's. Those two said that the role-playing sessions were useful and that more open-ended sharing among participants was needed.

Many of the comments are complementary to each other, e.g., "more role playing needed and less lecture" complements "role playing was useful." Some comments must simply be acknowledged by the instructor as things to consider in "fine-tuning" the course, e.g., "more privacy needed for small group course." A few comments suggest rather major change and they must be carefully weighed with the collective experience of training management, e.g., "instructors should be clear about a 'core' of items that are 'musts' for Emergency Management" or "course should be taught by someone experienced in EM at the state and local level so more applied knowledge can be offered."

Figure 2
Participant Critique of Training

Comments About the Training	Number of Participants Making Comment
• Testing for learning would have been useful.	1
• Reading material was excellent but not used by the instructors.	1
• Instructors should be clear about a "core" of items that are "musts" for the EM.	1
• Instructors assumed too much about what we already know; they should just go ahead and teach the essential material.	1
• Course should be taught by someone experienced in EM at the state and local level so more applied knowledge can be offered.	1
• Everything presented well.	1
• Course exercises should help with budgeting.	1
• Budget not advanced enough.	1
• Role playing was useful.	2
• Course should have been a bit shorter—too much input in a week.	1
• More privacy needed for small group work.	1
• Format good for exchanging ideas.	1
• More role playing needed and less lecture.	1
• More open-ended sharing needed.	2
• Course is taxing because it's designed for people with widely divergent needs.	1
• Handouts are repetitive and wasteful.	1
• Visuals are very beneficial.	1
• Social process ideas useful, especially as practiced in workshop format.	1
	20

5. Participant Reaction to Action Planning and Follow-up. The response of most participants to the action planning with follow-up was very positive (see Figure 3). It suggests, along with the actual achievements made by participants back on the job, that action planning should be seriously considered for other emergency management courses. It is clear that those who take the EM curriculum have widely differing needs depending upon their particular jobs and the constraints surrounding those jobs. Certainly this diversity of needs was true of the 11 participants in the Phase II session evaluated here.

Conclusion

The evaluator's exposure to EM field personnel has yielded a strong impression of job versatility within the emergency management field. Each person's job differs in focus, scope and detailed responsibility. Moreover, local conditions provide specific pressures to which each must respond individually.

Figure 3
Participant Reaction to
Action Planning and Follow-up

Comments About PAPA	Number of Participants Making Comments
• Very useful; good approach; great idea.	5
• Good idea for other FEMA courses.	1
• Suggest second follow-up several months later for longer-term results.	1
• Helpful in establishing what to do on the job one step at a time.	1
• Could have been discussed more in class.	1
• Difficult to project plans due to uncertainty of direction of work.	1

This extreme variability in job requirements, combined with equally extreme differences among EM personnel in professional background and experience, results in the phenomenon seen in this Phase II course just evaluated, i.e., extreme variability in what EM personnel planned to do back on the job and extreme differences in their reactions to the training.

This extreme variance in personal experience and job definition suggests that two conditions may be appropriate for much of the EM curriculum:

1. A "core" of major principles or tenets may be useful in helping EM personnel to master the enduring skills and knowledge areas. These core components should be the building blocks around which training is constructed.

2. At the same time, a good portion of actual training time should be devoted to facilitating the participant's definitions of their own needs and their sharing of problems and successful solutions on the job.

The Phase II course evaluated here was a rough approximation of such an attempt to combine these two conditions. Therefore, a radical departure from the present format seems unwarranted. The course manager and instructor should find the participant comments about the course helpful in planning subsequent sessions.

Matching Methods with the Nature of the Work

Each of the follow-up assessment approaches we have considered in this chapter has unique strengths and limitations. The evaluator's task is to choose the method or methods best suited to the type of performance being assessed, taking into account the given limitations of time, money and inconvenience to the operations of the organization.

The "decision tree" given below is offered as an aid in accomplishing this task. It is meant to provide focus to the evaluator's task, but it is not meant to pre-empt the use of more than one method. For example, an evaluator may wish to use both third-party observation and self-assessment to obtain as full and balanced a picture as possible of learning transfer.

Decision Tree
for
Selecting Follow-up Approaches

Can performance be readily observed
on the job by the trainer?

YES	NO
Use *direct observation* with performance criteria for making the assessment.	Can performance be readily observed on the job by the supervisor?

YES	NO
Use *third-party observation* with forms designed for the supervisor's use.	Can performance be accurately simulated?

YES	NO
Use *assessment center* and design a simulation to test performance.	Can work results be studied for a clear picture of performance effectiveness?

YES	NO
Use a *study of work results.* Develop criteria and assess the artifacts of the learner's work (reports, assembled products, sales volume, etc.)	Use *learner self-reporting* by providing the learner with a means for planning and conveying his or her actions on the job.

Summary

No matter how well training is executed and how well the learner performs in the context of training, if he or she cannot perform adequately in the actual performance environment, his or her training has yet to make a difference. The evaluator can use a variety of methods to assess the transfer of learning to the job: (1) direct observation; (2) third-party assessment; (3) assessment centers; (4) study of work results; and (5) learner self-reporting. The result of the evaluator's assessment can be useful to the trainer in modifying instruction and useful to the decision maker in determining what kind of investment to make in further training efforts.

Review of Progress

Evaluator Task #4: Assess the degree to which learning is transferred from training to actual performance situations.

Enabling Skills:
 • Ability to match follow-up assessment methods with different types of performance.
 • Ability to select or design criteria formats to assist in the assessment process.

Chapter note:
I am indebted to Ruth Salinger and Grazia Narkus-Kramer who developed the Participant Action Plan Approach at the U.S. Office of Personnel Management and introduced me to its versatility.

HANDOUT 1

Ideas for Action Items

Course: Dates:

Ideas I may wish to try out when I return to work, based on what I learned in this course.

Sources: Course objectives, class activities, handouts, conversations with others, etc.

HANDOUT 2

Guidelines
for
Writing Action Items

1. As you develop your items, be sure to recall your actual job setting as a way of testing the feasibility of the items.

2. Use action verbs which make the action item clear and purposeful. Some examples are listed here:

Intellectual Skill	*Motor Skill*	*Attitude*
Demonstrate	Adjust	Choose
Generate	Repair	Allow
Analyze	Replace	Cooperate
Evaluate	Calibrate	Accept
Derive	Operate	Agree

3. Ask yourself how you will know when you have performed each action item. Will it be obvious? Will you need to look for some indicator of success?

4. Can you anticipate problems in carrying out your items? What are they? What implications do they have for how you will carry out your planned activities?

Examples of action items:

- Generate a new budget proposal for the next fiscal year, using the principles set forth in the instructional booklet.

- Encourage employees to volunteer ideas for improving the work place.

- Repair the ventilating system in the engineering division, using the methods taught in the course.

- Think about when you will be able to begin implementing your action items. Note them under the following categories: (a) as the opportunity arises; (b) within 2 months; and (c) after 2 months.

HANDOUT 3

Action Plan

Name: A. Colby
Course Title: Emergency Management   Dates: May 2-5, 1982.

Action items	Start to implement (check if known)		
	Within 2 months	After 2 months	As Need Arises
1. Meet with budget analyst to discuss various items in budget so he may act effectively as my advocate at board of estimates budget meetings.		x	
2. Discuss possibility with staff of designing mail stuffers to be inserted in utility bills to promote emergency management issues before the public.	x		
3. Discuss with staff possibilities of gaining support from the key community figures to support budget efforts.	x		

Chapter 6

How Long Will It Last?

In the previous chapter, we considered the necessity of follow-up assessment in determining whether learning is transferred to actual performance settings, and we analyzed several methods for conducting follow-up assessment.

In this chapter, we look at a somewhat more complex variant of follow-up assessment—the assessment of performance over time.

In many cases, we should ask not only if the learner has transferred acquired knowledge or acquired skills to the actual performance setting but whether performance is maintained over a significant period of time.

We will consider two actual cases of training evaluation in which it was important to look at performance over an extended period of time, and in the process we will study one of the most respected and useful evaluation designs in use today. By the end of the chapter the reader should be able to design a time-series study for assessing learner performance over time and should be able to recognize situations in which a time-series design is appropriate.

Travel Voucher Training

One of the most tightly-regulated activities in government at any level is the authorization and reimbursement of government travel. Practically every municipality has its own set of guidelines, rules and forms, and usually any error in forms submission results in delay, extra paper processing and frustration for the traveler. These in turn mean more costly processing and lower morale.

One federal agency decided recently that too many errors and delays were occurring in the submission of travel vouchers. The travel section of the central finance office complained that its personnel were devoting excessive time to correcting vouchers which were not properly documented, not properly filled out or which contained mathematical errors. Agency personnel performing the travel complained they had to wait inordinate amounts of time for travel reimbursement.

Agency officials knew that vouchers were prepared by secretarial personnel who worked for dozens of organizational units. They had reasoned that the secretaries and clerks who prepared these vouchers could profit from training. By the same token, they knew the training had to be good to have an effect on performance, so they welcomed the advent of an outside evaluation team.

By the time the team was summoned, however, several months had passed since the first training session was administered to approximately 15 secretarial personnel. The evaluators arrived on the scene just before the second offering of the course which was held for another 15 secretaries and clerks. The evaluation team thoroughly examined course objectives, materials and test instruments and observed several classes of the training session. The evaluators concluded that the training was well conceived, well organized and well taught and frankly found it hard to conceive that those who took the course might continue to have difficulty in preparing travel vouchers back on the job.

Nevertheless, the evaluators reviewed stacks of processed vouchers to see whether they could discover a detectable improvement in voucher preparation due to training. They discovered instead there were too few vouchers submitted over a six-week period following training to draw clear conclusions.

The evaluators then turned to an assessment method which the author has called the "over-the-shoulder" method. The evaluators interviewed secretarial personnel who had taken the first training session almost six months earlier. The strategy was to assess whether those learners had maintained their performance over an extended period of time. Several persons interviewed said they had found the course to be excellent and that they had come away feeling confident in their knowledge of voucher preparation rules and processes. Over the months which followed, however, most of them had processed only a few vouchers and found that much of what they learned had been forgotten. Consequently, they fell back into old habits of calling the finance travel unit for assistance or of submitting vouchers without being certain they were properly completed or documented.

Here then was an instance of performance failing to endure over time. The training was excellent; the training participants who were fortunate enough to have vouchers waiting for them upon their return to the job could process them with a high degree of success. By and large, though, most of the gains made in the training sessions were washed out over time through lack of opportunity for task repetition and reinforcement. Through empirical observation and experimentation, learning psychologists have documented the usual effect of time on learning which is not practiced frequently. Typically, the learner loses a great deal of skill or information very rapidly after training. This initial loss is followed by a more gradual deterioration of performance until the learner retains only a small fragment of what he or she originally learned.

Thus, it was not surprising that the same personnel who did so well on the travel voucher course post-test had lost most of their acquired ability within six months due to lack of practice.

In this case, the evaluators recommended that one of two actions be taken by the agency: either develop job aids which would keep essential voucher preparation information at the secretary's fingertips, or move voucher preparation in its entirety to the central processing office. What eventually occurred with respect to travel vouchers in this agency will be discussed in the next chapter where we will consider the cost and relative value of training.

Photocomposition Training

This next case provides a classic example of the need for evaluation over an extended time period. Here it was not so much what the evaluators did but what they learned from their efforts that provides lessons for us.

The training in question took the form of a course for photocomposition operators given at a federal installation which prepares large volumes of printed material for publication. These operators type material onto word processors according to given formats. The course was offered by a vendor who claimed that he could significantly increase the keyboard skills of the photocomposition operators. He predicted among other results a gain in speed of at least 15 percent and reduction of errors by 50 percent. These were attractive claims, and so the agency decided to try the course on a portion of its veteran photocomposition work force. It also decided to obtain outside help to assess the value of this course.

The evaluation team discovered some fundamental problems at the outset. First, the agency officials had requested volunteers for the training, and of a force of more than 30 operators, only nine eventually attended the training sessions. The evaluators had hoped for a larger class so that extremely poor or unusually outstanding performance would not affect group scores too drastically. But more important, they had hoped for a random selection of operators for the training so that they could reasonably assume that the trainees and their fellow operators were comparable. It is conceivable, for instance, that those who volunteered were more highly motivated to perform well and thus might benefit from training to a significantly greater degree than would those who did not volunteer. In fact, the evaluators found that the volunteer group clearly outscored their peers on a pretest measure of photocomposition accuracy and speed.

Of course, the evaluation team had to function within the constraints imposed and did its best to take precise measures of performance. It assisted agency personnel in developing equivalent tests which were highly accurate approximations of work done on the job. These tests were administered both to the training participants and the control group just prior to training, at the completion of training, and from four to six weeks after training.

The results from these tests were both exciting and frustrating. As Figure 1 depicts, the training participants from the third work shift showed a dramatic gain in accuracy on both the post test and the follow-up test. On the other hand, there was a puzzling decrease in follow-up scores of the first work shift training participants and a problematic gain in performance by the control group on shift two.

Taken all together, the trained group of operators improved its overall performance by almost 10 percent while the control group declined in its performance by almost 6 percent. Unfortunately (or perhaps mercifully), the evaluation was terminated at that point. There lay the promise of perhaps a 10 percent improvement in operator performance which could amount to a savings for the agency of more than $165,000 over five years. But no one could be sure whether (a) those who did not take the training would derive as much from it in a later session as the original volunteers; (b) the gain in performance by the volunteer group was real, considering how group scores fluctuated over the three tests; or (c) four to six weeks was a sufficient time delay for measuring the endurance of skill acquisition. Ultimately, the agency decided not to continue contracting for the course. This may have been the most appropriate decision since agency officials did not believe they could afford to experiment with it again using a more rigorous experimental design.

Figure 1

**Comparison of average error rates between
shifts 1, 2 and 3, trainees and control group,
for the three work samples taken.**

TRAINEES _____

CONTROLS ----------------------------

	Shift 1			Shift 2			Shift 3		
Pre	Post	Follow-up	Pre	Post	Follow-up	Pre	Post	Follow-up

ERRORS PER 100 EMS — .40, .30, .20, .10

Time-Series Design

Fortunately, we have the luxury of hindsight and can project what an appropriate evaluation design would look like for the photocomposition training. We begin by achieving a better representation of the work force by randomly selecting operators from each shift, perhaps twice as many as those who volunteered. Then we establish a baseline measure of the key production variables, in this case accuracy and speed. As depicted in Figure 2, we would take several pre-course measures in order to establish a definite tendency to perform. We would also take several measures after training to establish as conclusively as possible (a) whether we have a real gain; and (b) whether the gain holds up over time. The cost of these evaluations must of course be considered, but where hundreds of thousands of dollars might be saved, it seems a reasonable course of action.

Figure 2

Time-Series with Controls Design

	Pretest	Treatment	Post-Test
Exp Group	T1 T2 T3	X	T4 T5 T6
Controls	T1 T2 T3		T4 T5 T6

This evaluation paradigm, called a time-series with controls design, is a cadillac among experimental designs. It provides safeguards against measurement error and fluctuations of performance caused by intervening events. The question is whether the potential gain is great enough to justify the expenditures of time and human resources that are implied by the time-series design. Of course, hindsight is not as useful as foresight, but the agency with the photocomposition work force would certainly have been justified had it invested at the start in a time-series with controls design.

Implementing a Time-Series Design

Now let's consider the design of a time-series study in detail. There are four basic things to accomplish:
1. Select treatment group; and select control group (optional).
2. Select appropriate measures and measurement points.
3. Formulate a measurement plan.
4. Design a management plan to make the evaluation work.

We will use another actual case study for practical examples of each implementation step.

A large federal agency had conducted a major needs analysis of its auditor-evaluation staff of over 1,500 individuals. It found that the single most prominent problem cited by its professional work force was poor communication at the project level. Based upon the needs analysis, the agency contracted with a private consultant to plan and deliver a week-long workshop on interpersonal communication skills. The agency hoped to train its entire professional work force over a two-year period through a continuous series of these workshops.

The agency was willing to commit a considerable portion of its human resource development budget to the objective of increasing interpersonal communication skills on the presumption that better project team communication would result in more efficient and effective audit-evaluation results. However, it wanted some reliable evidence that the training would be effectively transferred to the job.

As a consequence of the agency's concern with learning transfer, a follow-up assessment was planned. It was to involve trained observers who would make on-site assessments of communication skills usage during meetings of project teams which consisted of one or more individuals who had participated in the communication skills training. The plan was admirable from a theoretical standpoint in that observers could make very reliable assessments of the learners' abilities to use their skills on the job. However, the plan broke down in execution. Too many managers and auditor-evaluators found the presence of these trained observers threatening or overly inconvenient and therefore refused to cooperate in their efforts to observe teams in action.

This refusal to cooperate with the evaluator could have been remedied by top management had it chosen to intervene. It did not. Ultimately, the evaluator relied upon paper and pencil instruments to collect self-reported data. The instruments were well designed and the data were reasonably useful. But no one was ever able to establish independently whether many of the learners were able to use their newly acquired behaviors effectively in the privacy of their work groups. Let us use this actual evaluation experience as a departure point and again, with the luxury of hindsight, project a way in which not only the transfer of learning to the job can be assessed but the endurance of performance over time as well.

Step 1: Select Treatment Group

In this case, our treatment group can be any random collection of auditor-evaluators, providing the work these individuals do is representative of the work most members of that work force perform. We want a representative group so we can treat it as a valid sample of a population. Thus, if this group successfully transfers its learning to the work setting, we can infer by generalization that most of the auditor-evaluators will. For practical purposes we use the first two groups who are assigned to be trained as our sample.

Step 2: Select Appropriate Measures and Measurement Points

Because a pervasive need for interpersonal communication skill development was well-defined through a needs analysis, we don't have to establish a baseline of performance before training. In this case, we may safely assume that for practical purposes everyone can noticeably improve his or her communications skills through training. However, we do need to define what criteria we will use to measure performance at the end of training and at subsequent points in time after training (six week intervals).

We decide that measurement criteria should be taken from the skills model which formed the basis of training instruction. In this model we find skills such as self-disclosing, probing, confronting, clarifying, checking, centering, appreciating and summarizing. For each skill, role modeling is provided in the context of the course. Each role model episode, either demonstrated directly by the instructor or shown by videotape or film, provides a standard by which the learner's skill can be assessed.

Step 3: Formulate a Measurement Plan

Since we are trying to assess the relatively enduring effect training has on performance, we must devise a way to obtain repeated measures over time. Some organizations routinely collect data on critical indicators of job performance. In those cases, the evaluator can simply appropriate those data for his or her own purposes. However, where no measurements are routinely taken, a plan for data collection must be initiated. That plan should meet the following criteria:

1. Data collection activities should intrude as little as possible on normal tasks performed by operating personnel.

2. Data collection activities should occur as routinely as possible.

3. Measures should be unambiguous and easily recorded.

4. Measures should provide information on the most important characteristics of performance, e. g., timeliness or accuracy.

5. Data, once collected, should be coded and analyzed as quickly as possible so that problems in data collection can be identified and rectified promptly.

6. Measures and data collection methods should be revised promptly to meet unanticipated consequences, e.g., disagreement between observers on criteria for performance or quality of observed performance.

Measurement Plan Applied

We know we would have great difficulty in observing interpersonal communication skills in the context of the job due to the sensitivity of the individuals involved. We also know that third-party observation is not feasible for the same reason. Moreover, there is no visible product which we can study as an indicator of learning transfer. However, we can use an assessment center to measure skill levels directly.

Our plan is to devise a series of role playing encounters in which the learner is expected to use the interpersonal communication skills taught in training. The encounter involves a trained participant who role-plays in such a way as to set the stage for each behavior taught. A trained observer records the learner's behaviors as he or she interacts with the trained participant and rates the learner on each behavior according to its appropriateness and effectiveness.

Let's consider the measurement plan in greater detail by using the six criteria described above as guidelines.

1. By bringing the learner out of the work setting rather than try-

ing to observe him or her interacting on the job, we succeed in avoiding undesirable intrusion into the intimate work environment.

2. We can establish a reasonable routine for learner assessment by scheduling well in advance. In this case, we may wish to make arrangements for each learner to visit the assessment center once every six weeks at a time convenient both to the learner and to the assessment personnel.

3. By using the training models for each skill, we have an implicit standard for performance. The observer can use a checksheet as simple as the following once he has been trained to assess the various communication behaviors:

Skill	No opportunity to use	Used at Approp. Time	Used Effectively	Comments
Self-disclosing				
Probing				
Confronting				
Clarifying				
Checking				
Centering				
Appreciating				
Summarizing				
Other				

4. In this case, our measures are no more and no less than the very behaviors we wish to assess. Other aspects of the learner's performance are deliberately excluded in the assessment center exercise.

5. We should make certain that the observer always records the assessment on the supplied form and that he or she completes it on the spot. This type of observation assessment is too detailed to be kept accurately in one's mind for any length of time after the performance.

6. We should plan on reviewing the completed observation forms regularly. If we have more than one trained observer, we may wish to have them rate the same learner simultaneously on occasion to make sure they are still recording with high inter-rater reliability. We should also be checking to see if our trained role player is providing all the appropriate behavioral cues for the skills we wish to observe the learner demonstrating.

Step 4: Formulate a Management Plan

This step could be tagged "greasing the wheels" since it adds nothing to the evaluation in the way of input or output data but is essential to the smooth functioning of the endeavor. The management plan is a way of providing the motivation necessary to keep key personnel committed to making the evaluation possible.

In our case, we are dependent upon both the learner who exercises considerable job autonomy as an auditor-evaluator and agency managers who set priorities for the work place. We decide to make the assessment center visit as pleasant an experience as possible for the learner with a cheerful decor, pleasant informal exchanges and positive verbal reinforcement of his or her willingness to go through the exercises. We also place a routine call as a reminder of the appointment shortly before the agreed-upon time.

We also communicate periodically with the managers of the auditor-evaluators who are participating in the follow-up assessment. Our purpose is to remind them of top management's commitment to the program. Occasionally, we provide the appropriate executive with a written statement which he or she has the option of presenting to his or her managers at meetings regarding the continued importance of supporting the assessment activity.

There is no universal formula for a management plan. Many successful individuals have intuitive approaches to working with others that accomplish the same results. We are attempting simply to make explicit an element of successful management which can assist the evaluator to negotiate what can be a difficult process. Performing an evaluation of this type is inevitably complex and difficult because the evaluator necessarily relies on the cooperation of many others for the integrity and success of his or her study. A management plan should support the evaluator by treating the human dimension or, if you like, the motivational dimension of the evaluation activity.

Hypothetical Results

There are a number of results which might emanate from the follow-up assessment considered here. Let's consider one very plausible scenario (see Figure 3 below). Here we see that at the end of the first six weeks back on the job, learners performed slightly better than at the conclusion of training—a good indication that they were using their newly acquired skills.

Figure 3

Mean Effectiveness of Interpersonal Communications Skills Through Simulation

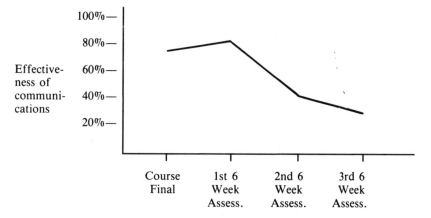

However, the next two follow-up assessments (2nd and 3rd) show a sharp and continuous decline in skill performance. This suggests that after a time, many learners stopped using the skills taught them and, therefore, their facility in using them declined rapidly.

These are extremely useful results for the trainer and for management. They suggest that without some type of reinforcement, learners are not sufficiently motivated to continue using their newly acquired skills long enough for them to become habitual or second-nature. We might recommend, in a situation like this one, that the assessment center concept be continued, but augmented to provide instructional feedback to the learner on his or her observed performance. Videotaped sessions, replayed for the learner, can have profoundly reinforcing effects on the learner's desire to keep using and improving his or her use of interpersonal communication skills.

Once such an intervention is implemented, we might find, through continued assessment, dramatically improved performance (see Figure 4 below). It is likely that performance would once again deteriorate once assessment center activities (including videotape play-backs) were discontinued, but the deterioration should not be nearly as severe as that which would have occurred after the first six-week assessment period. Rather, it should plateau at a level of acceptable performance.

Figure 4

**Mean Effectiveness of Interpersonal
Communication Skills Before
and After Video-Feedback Sessions**

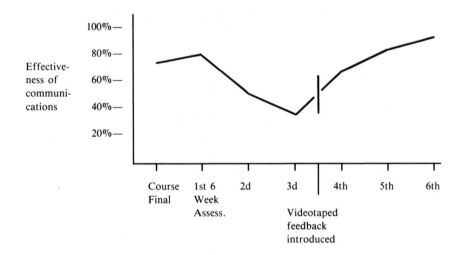

When to Use Time-Series Assessment

The use of time-series design to measure not only the transfer of learning but the endurance of performance is more costly than most other assessment methods—more costly in terms of time, resources and management commitment. Therefore, it should be used only when simpler methods would fail to do the job. We can generalize about those cases in which time-series assessment may be the only truly adequate means of evaluation:

1. Whenever mastery of learning will only occur with the application of skills or knowledge over time.

There are many skills, such as the interpersonal communication skills described above, which cannot be truly mastered within the time-frame of a training course or program. Many supervisory and managerial skills fall into this category, as do many complex technical skills. Whenever one has reason to fear that skills may not be improved or that they may deteriorate over time (probably due to their not being applied effectively in the actual performance setting), time-series assessment should be seriously considered.

2. Whenever occasions for performance are known to be intermittent or rare.

There are some skills and bodies of knowledge which are extremely important to the user but which are seldom called upon. Examples of these types of skill and knowledge are responding to nuclear accidents and evacuating communities. Simulation exercises are standard means both for providing practice and for assessing performance in cases such as these.

3. Whenever change is likely to be subtle or difficult to detect but is nevertheless important.

When we considered the agency which trained its photocomposition operators to improve their keyboard techniques, we noted that a small increase in proficiency could result in a substantial cost savings to the agency over time. Yet the only way one could have determined true and enduring effects of training on performance was by using an extended time-series assessment.

In the actual case, the evaluation team observed far too much fluctuation in performance to generalize about the effects of training. One follow-up measurement of performance was inadequate. Interestingly, the contractor had projected a gain in speed of at least 15 percent and a reduction in errors by 50 percent. Had a lasting effect been as little as 2 percent gain in speed and a 10 percent reduction in errors, the savings could have paid for the training several times over.

Summary

In this chapter we have analyzed time-series assessment as the chief method for measuring the endurance of performance over time. It is, by comparison with other methods, a relatively costly undertaking. Whenever mastery can only be expected to occur over a long period of time, whenever occasions for performance are intermittent or rare and whenever change is likely to be subtle or difficult to detect, the time-series approach is advisable.

Review of Progress

Evaluator Task #5: Assess the endurance of learned performance over time.

Enabling Skills:
- Ability to design a time-series study for assessing learner performance over time
- Ability to recognize situations in which time-series assessment is appropriate

---

Chapter 7

Is Training Worth The Investment?

One of the most common characteristics of training operations in both the private and public sectors is their vulnerability. When a company or agency possesses sufficient funds to cover all its recurrent needs, decision makers typically support the organization's training program, sometimes with more generosity than is truly needed. But when the economy shrinks, and a business loses profits or an agency has its allocations cut, those same decision makers frequently sacrifice large chunks of the training program in the name of cost reduction.

The training director is often unable to exert sufficient influence to save even those parts of the program which are essential to the proper conduct of business in the organization. The director's pleas are largely ignored, and his or her staff (what remains of it) is left wondering whether their services are really valued by the organization.

In the long run, the savings gained by these cuts in the training program are often totally offset by loss due to decreased effectiveness in job performance. This shortsightedness on the part of management shouldn't surprise us. Major segments of U.S. industry have for years sacrificed essential long-term investments in basic research and plant and equipment modernization to the short-term goal of immediate profit. Investment in qualified personnel through training and development programs is another long-term investment which has been regularly sacrificed.

Now that American manufacturers have been overtaken in so many areas of production by Japanese and European corporations, U.S. executives are beginning to understand the effects of their long-term neglect. Moreover, unions have been pushing harder lately for job-related training in their realization that rapid changes in technology threaten to make the skills of large portions of today's workers obsolete in a few years. Thus the stage is set for a more positive response by decision makers to the trainer's argument for his or her portion of the organization's budget.

But in many cases the trainer has no argument to make, other than to echo old assertions that training is, after all, essential to an organization's well being. Unfortunately, it is not enough to show that training is well conceived and well taught, or even that it has been shown to have a tangible impact on job performance. What the trainer lacks is the ability to lay out for the decision maker the probable consequences of a diminished training effort—loss of productivity, decreased quality in goods or services and (frequently the most important effect) loss of capital.

What follows are guides for helping the trainer or the evaluator to project:

1. The cost of training.
2. The costs of alternatives to training.
3. The probable benefits of training.

When the reader has finished this chapter, he or she will be able to calculate the cost of training, and be able to project probable gain or loss to the organization on the basis of either supporting or sacrificing a training effort. Of course, the ability to project the value of training relative to its cost may be used to market new training efforts, not merely to justify present programs. Therefore, it is an ability appropriate for the flush times as well as the austere.

Calculating the Cost of Training

There are several potential costs associated with training. Often the trainer or evaluator will not have direct access to many of these costs (facility costs, equipment costs, etc.) but must obtain figures or reliable estimates from his or her organization's budget operation. Usually, all of these cost categories can be accounted for with little guess work.

Trainee Cost. Most commonly, organizations pay their people while they are in training, regardless of whether the training is entry-level or advanced. And typically, training is conducted during normal work hours, so that the trainee is not able to perform at his or her regular job. Thus, every hour the trainee is in training may cost an organization the equivalent of an hour's earnings for that individual. Moreover, those earnings need to be taken as a total compensation package, for the organization's commitment to the individual may include paid insurance premiums, social security contributions, matched retirement contributions, etc. In a very real sense, an employee's time is worth more than the compensation he or she earns (at least in private enterprise) for he or she is expected to contribute to the profit of the company. However, the compensation package provides at least a convenient means for calculating trainee costs.

For example, the trainee cost for a group of 20 engineers attending a three-day seminar would be the sum of the three days' salary for each of the 20 engineers. If we averaged the actual salaries plus calculable benefits we might get something like the following:

No. trainees	x	Avg. daily compensation	x	Length of training	=	Trainee cost
20		$117.50		3 days		$7050 (20 x $117.50 x 3)

Instructor Cost. Just as trainee compensation should be calculated as a training cost, so should instructor compensation. However, more may be involved than just the hours and days the instructor gives to actual training activities. In addition, all preparation time should be calculated. So, for example, if an instructor requires five days' preparation for a three-day seminar, instructor cost amounts to eight days of compensation:

No. instr's	x	Avg. daily compensation	x	(Length of training	+	Length of prep.)	=	Instructor cost
1		$121.00		3		5		$968

Instructional Development Cost. If an organization contracts for training, the cost of developing the instructional format and materials may be lumped together with all the other costs the contractor will attempt to recover. If, on the other hand, the instruction is developed in-house, then its cost needs to be calculated. That can be done by keeping track of both the time expended by the developer and the cost expended in development of software, e.g., transparencies, videotapes, simulators, etc. A calculation of development costs could look like the following:

Daily comp. of developer(s)	x	Length of development	+	Material cost of software	=	Instr. development cost
$121.00		15 days		$1700		$3515

The actual cost of instructional development can be treated differently than trainee and instructor costs insofar as the training will be used repeatedly. For example, if the developed instructional format and software were used three times, then the development cost assigned to any one training session would be one-third the total development cost. The more frequent the use of the training, the more economical the investment in instructional development becomes.

Instr. development cost	÷	Number of sessions	=	Development cost per session
$3515		3		1171.67

Materials Cost. Frequently, trainers use "off-the-shelf" material, i.e., material prepackaged by a vendor for a number of potential users. The cost of these materials as well as the cost of instrumental materials such as pads of paper, pens, news sheet and the like can be subsumed under this category. So can other perishables such as meals and coffee when they are supplied at no cost to the trainee.

Purchased software	+	Instrumental materials	+	Perishables	=	Materials cost
$1200		$35		$60		$1295

Equipment and Related Personnel Costs. Some training requires equipment that must be purchased and then maintained. In other instances, training can be scheduled around the availability of equipment in normal use by the organization. For example, training for brakemen may involve the occasional usage of a locomotive and a set of railroad cars. The usage may be for all practical purposes cost-free if it is during "idle" time on the engineer's and foreman's work schedule. More likely, however, each training event would have to be scheduled as any other work assignment for those personnel. Therefore, the wage or salary cost as well as the cost of using the locomotive and rolling stock would have to be calculated.

Personnel cost per hour	x	No. hours	+	(Equipment cost per hour	x	No. hours)	=	Equipment and related pers. cost
1 Engineer:								
$15		6		$146		6		$1020
1 Foreman:								
$10		6						

In instances where equipment must be purchased specifically for training, the cost can be amortized over the number of training sessions or number of years it will be used, depending upon whether you are calculating an annual training cost or a cost per training course or program.

(Actual equipment cost	÷	Anticipated length of service)	+	Yearly maintenance	=	Amortized Equipment cost
$350,000		10 years		$7000		$42,000

Facilities Cost. There are a variety of approaches to calculating the cost of a facility. In the rare instances where a building or special structure is designed and constructed primarily for training, the cost can be amortized over its functional lifetime, with a maintenance cost added on, if appropriate (as with purchased equipment).

If training is conducted within a facility that is used for several other functions, then the appropriate fraction of that facility's cost should be ascribed to the training.

Facilities yearly cost	x	% Time used for training	=	Facilities cost
$4200		15%		$630

Contract Cost. This is the cost for services rendered by a contractor. Typically, it involves cost above and beyond those already described in this chapter. If equipment, facilities or supplies are involved, the contractor is normally expected to set forth an itemized inventory of those costs as well as development costs and personnel costs. In addition, he or she will stipulate overhead costs and other incidentals such as travel, per diem and special fees to be paid by the contractor in accomplishing his or her work.

It can be useful (and it is now required under certain conditions by state and federal government) to show the breakdown of a contractor's full cost package with a projected cost for performing the same or comparable service in-house.

Comparison of Contractor and In-House Training Costs

	Cost of course development	+	Cost of equipmnt/ materials	+	Instructor cost	+	Over-head	+	Contract = Admin.	Comparative Training Cost
Course 1										
Contractor	$750		$360		$5000		$2500		$100	$8710
In-house	$1200		$360		$3200		-		-	$4760
Course 2										
Contractor	$1800		$200		$4500		$2250		$150	$8900
In-house	$6500		$220		$3700		-		-	$10420

The first course shown above reflects the tendency for personnel expenses to be more economical when used from within the organization. (Note the "Instructor cost" column.) This presumes that the appropriate skills or knowledge can be found from within. The second course reflects the tendency for development to cost more when done in-house. (Note the "Cost of course development" column.) This is true when no particular expertise or prior experience in the appropriate subject matter exists within the organization but does exist within the contractor's resources.

Travel and Per Diem Cost. For in-house training, travel and per diem are often of no consequence. But for training away from the work location, they can become serious cost factors. Let's reconsider the Course 2 example given above. We noted that the in-house option was more costly due to the need for a great deal more instructional development than the contractor would require. Now let's assume the contractor had proposed holding the training in his or her own city rather than on-site: It could change the picture dramatically:

Round trip air fare per person	x	No. of trainees	+	Per diem rate	x	No. of trainees	x	No. of days	=	Travel/ per diem costs
$78		15		$45		15		5		$4545

Now when we compare the contractor with the in-house cost, we have the following:

Comparative training cost	+	Travel/ per diem	=	Total training cost	
$8900		$4545		$13,445	Contractor
$10,420				$10,420	In-house

Estimating the Net Benefit or Loss of Training

It should be evident now that the trainer or evaluator can calculate the cost of training, albeit with the assistance of people who have access to certain fiscal data which the trainer ordinarily does not have at his or her fingertips. More challenging is the art of estimating the relative benefits of training, but it can be done. It simply takes imaginative thinking and the will to set reasonable values for those factors which influence cost, e.g., error rates, volume of output, absenteeism, managerial knowledge and skills.

Cost of Alternatives to Training

You may recall from Chapter 6 a description of an evaluation dealing with travel voucher training. The evaluation team had discovered that many of the secretaries taking the course were unable to perform as well months later as they were at the end of the course. The considerable length of time between vouchers submitted back on the job had led to serious deterioration of learning.

Pursuant to the evaluation team's discovery that the effects of training were not enduring, agency decision makers began to consider ways to supplement training with job aides, hoping that the combination would result in improved performance. At this point, the evaluation team developed a method (see Figure 1) for determining whether the voucher training could be justified in terms of cost-effectiveness, even if with the job aides it evoked flawless voucher preparation on the part of the secretarial work force.

1. First, the team had finance office personnel record the extra time they spent to process vouchers with errors (Figure 1, Step 1). They did this over a four-week period. The time spent averaged 16 minutes per voucher.

2. The team tabulated the number of vouchers with errors submitted to the finance office in that same four-week period (Step 2). They counted 195 vouchers.

3. The total extra time for the four-week period was computed simply by multiplying the average time per voucher times the number of vouchers (Step 3)—3,120 minutes or 52 hours.

4. To estimate the extra time required to rework these vouchers in a year, the team again multiplied (see Step 4), in this case the number of hours in the four-week period times 13 (the number of four-week periods in a year). This yielded an estimate of 676 hours.

5. In Step 5, the team multiplied the hours spent in rework times the average hourly salary of the finance office personnel who reworked the vouchers (approximately $6 per hour). This produced an estimated yearly cost in salary of $4,056 to process vouchers with errors.

Figure 1
Analysis of Gain or Loss Due to Training

Step 1

Extra time spent by finance office to process vouchers with errors:
16 minutes/voucher

Step 2

Total number of vouchers with errors submitted in four-week period: *195*

Step 3

Total extra time (four-week period): *52 hours*

Step 4

Total extra time per year: *676 hours*

Step 5

Yearly salary costs of examiners to process vouchers with errors: *$4,056*

Step 6

Cost to train 15 secretaries (one class); includes secretary and instructor salaries, materials and course development: *$3,600*

Step 7

Cost to train 150 secretaries in 10 classes (number of secretaries submitting vouchers with errors): *$36,000*

Step 8

Average length of tenure for secretarial staff: *3 years*

Step 9

Amortized cost of training per year: *$12,000*

Step 10

Gain or loss through training:
training cost	=	$12,000
cost of not training	=	$4,056
loss due to training	=	$7,944

6. In Step 6, the cost of training 15 secretaries or one class in voucher preparation was verified as $3,600.

7. To train all the secretaries who submitted vouchers with errors (150 of them), as Step 7 shows, 10 comparable classes would be required at a cost of $36,000.

8. Step 8 involves reviewing the length of tenure for the agency's secretarial force. It was found to be approximately three years.

9. In Step 9, the projected cost of training the secretarial force of 150 is divided by three. If the learning endured over time, the training could be considered effective for an average period of three years for the entire group. Thus the annual cost would be amortized to $12,000.

10. Step 10 involves comparing the projected training cost with the projected cost of *not* training. In this case, the assumption is made that the cost to the finance office in reworking claims will remain constant, i.e., approximately $4,056. This cost is acceptable since the alternative is a training effort at almost three times the expense of reworking the claims. Moreover, the ratio would probably be far less favorable for training in actuality since this projection assumes that the training effort would be sufficient to reduce the rework rate to virtually nothing—and keep it there.

Ultimately, the evaluation team recommended that the agency centralize voucher processing and add one person to the finance staff to absorb the additional work. This action would result in more efficient voucher preparation, less frustration for travelers and a substantial cost avoidance to the agency in the form of training not conducted for the secretarial personnel.

The method used to project the cost of voucher rework in the finance office is not perfect. For example, the team worked on the assumption that the four-week results used for assessment were typical of what one would find over almost any four-week period during a year. This assumption may not be accurate. Nevertheless, it offered a rough gauge for computation, and the ultimate results were so dramatically in favor of not training, even a large difference in performance would not have changed the results.

Pricing Effects of Substandard Performance

In training offered for many technical specialities, potential cost savings can be estimated from studying the effects of substandard performance on the job. The results may be waste, inefficiency, failure to meet deadlines and lost customers—and each of these can be given a reasonable dollar value. For example:

1. The person who orders material can provide accurate figures for the original value of material. From that, waste percentage can be calculated into dollars lost.

2. Inefficiency can be translated into a percentage of a person's work by an industrial psychologist or engineer, and from that a portion of salary or wage can be projected as loss.

3. Failure to meet deadlines can be translated into lost profit by sales or contract management personnel who are in a position to see the cumulative effects of missed deadlines in terms of reduced or cancelled orders.

In effect, wherever the person's work results in the actual making or disposition of a product, or wherever it amounts to providing a direct service to a client or customer, its value can be closely estimated or precisely calculated, just as the extra work required to correct travel vouchers in our example was timed and weighed by worker salary.

Cost-Benefit Analysis of Manager and Executive Development

But let's consider a more challenging case. How can we attribute a specific monetary value to job behavior which is one or more steps removed from observable results? We usually cannot draw direct cause and effect relationships between an executive's policy making or communication skills and such identifiable outcomes as volume of sales or rates of production.

Here we must depend upon some substitute for the direct computation of loss or gain. To be useful to us, it must be consistent, rational and conservative in its method of value attribution.

Affixing Value to Performance

To assign value to something which we think will improve performance, we first must assign a value to that performance. If we believe that a course in time management will improve a manager's ability to plan and prioritize his or her tasks, to assign a value to the course, we must first attribute a value to "planning and prioritizing tasks."

That may seem a bit trivial, and it would be if we were to focus only on that one specific dimension of a manager's performance. In fact, in order to assign any reasonable value to a specific skill, we must assign values to the entirety of the job skills and knowledge as they are evidenced in actual performance. This may seem just as impractical as attributing a value to one specific behavior, or a small portion of a manager's behavior. However, to assign values to the major skills and knowledge areas of a manager's job becomes eminently defensible when we wish to judge the value of *any* training the manager may undertake.

Figure 2 depicts a set of knowledge areas and skills which fairly circumscribe the job of physical resource manager as it is defined in one particular organization. To assign values to these knowledge areas and skills we can do the following:

1. We can ask incumbents of this position how they rate the relative importance of each area.

2. We can ask senior managers who must supervise these incumbents to rate the relative importance of each.

3. We can ask both sets of managers to rate relative importance and combine their responses.

Figure 2
Major Knowledge and Skill Areas
for Physical Resource Management with
Importance Weightings Based on Ratio Data

Knowledge Areas	Importance Weightings
1. Facilities and construction management	3
2. Major capital repair and maintenance management procedures	4
3. Property and fund accountability systems	1.5
4. Travel proposal system	1

Skills	
1. Problem definition	2
2. Priority setting	5
3. Program planning	4
4. Program execution and coordination	5
5. Program review and evaluation	2
6. Interpersonal interactions	3
7. Supervisory activities	1.5

In order to project an accurate estimate of the relative importance of each knowledge and skill area, each rater is asked to choose the least important item first and give it a rating of "1." Then every other item is rated as a ratio of that item of least importance. Note in Figure 2 that the knowledge area called "travel proposal system" was judged by the rater to be the least important item in the physical resource manager position (it was given a "1"). By constrast, "priority setting" and "program execution and coordination" were judged to be five times as important. Theoretically, there is no upper limit to the number given to important items.

However, as long as we have limited knowledge areas and skills to those which define the job in its major aspects, we can expect that the range will not exceed "10" on a ratio scale.

Let's assume now that the importance weightings shown in Figure 2 (which represent the rating of one person) are averaged together with weightings of several raters (see Figure 3). Now we have a basis for attributing monetary value to each major knowledge and skill area. We do this by adding all the weighted item ratings together and then dividing each weighted item by the total. Figure 3 shows, for example, that the total weighted ratings amount to 37.4. Note that the item, "travel proposal system," is still the lowest weighted of all the items, now averaged at 1.3 from the ratings of several persons. Its percentage of the total average weighted ratings (those for all 11 items) is 3.5 percent (1.3 divided by 37.4).

One step remains in calculating a monetary value for this item. We simply multiply the percentage of total weighted ratings represented by the selected item (in this case, 3.5 percent) by the individual's salary ($36,000). The operation yields $1,260. This means that in terms of the incumbent's salary, this knowledge area is worth approximately 3.5 percent of that salary, or $1,260. Figure 3 shows the values for all position items.

One may question the use of salary for establishing the relative value of a knowledge area or skill. The fact is that salary is the most visible and measurable means for attributing value. Were we to attempt to project the value of a knowledge area or skill on the basis of "true" worth to an organization, we would first have to establish exhaustive cause and effect relationships between what individuals have accomplished for the organization in terms of the knowledge areas and skills and what effects their accomplishments had on product sales, rate of production, amount of waste, etc. Because we are dealing with managerial actions which are one or more steps removed from most "shop floor" activities, we cannot in all reality perform this feat. Salary, on the other hand, remains a stable indicator of worth and lends itself nicely to value attribution attempts.

In the example depicted in Figure 3, we used salary as a base for attributing values to each major knowledge and skill area. We could as easily have used a multiplier of salary to more closely approximate the "true" monetary worth of an individual to the organization. For example, in bidding for contracts, it is common for an organization to show an employee's salary with 50 percent to 100

Figure 3
Dollar Values for Major
Knowledge and Skill Areas for a
Physical Resource Manager

Knowledge Areas	Average Weighted Rating	% of Total Weighted Ratings	*Portion of Average Annual Salary
1. Facilities and construction management	3.2	8.6	$3,096
2. Major capital repair and maintenance management procedures	4.3	11.5	4,140
3. Property and fund accountability systems	1.7	4.5	1,620
4. Travel proposal system	1.3	3.5	1,260
Skills			
1. Problem definition	1.9	5.1	1,836
2. Priority setting	4.4	11.8	4,248
3. Program planning	5.2	13.9	5,004
4. Program execution and coordination	7.3	19.5	7,020
5. Program review and evaluation	2.2	5.9	2,124
6. Interpersonal interactions	4.1	11.0	3,960
7. Supervisory activities	2.8	7.5	2,700
TOTAL	37.4	**102.8	**$37,008

*   Based on average annual salary of $36,000

** Exceeds 100 percent due to rounding error

percent added on as overhead. This overhead usually covers the administrative costs of carrying the employee on the company roll plus a profit margin. Therefore, we could assign a multiplier of 1.5 or 2 to the salary. Thus, from our example above, the knowledge area, "travel proposal system," originally valued at $1,260, would instead be valued at $1,890 (using 1.5 as a multiplier) or $2,520 (using 2 as a multiplier).

Measuring Potential Value of Training

Once we have attributed values to each of the major knowledge and skill areas, we need to consider two other important factors in assessing the potential value of training: (1) the individual's ability in each area; and (2) the degree to which a particular training experience can improve that ability. Whether we ask the individuals to rate themselves or we ask their immediate superior to rate them, we must obtain a usable rating of the person's ability in each of the knowledge and skill areas. This rating must be relatable both to the level of competence called for in the given knowledge and skill areas and the level of competence for which a given training experience is designed. So, what we require is a standard rating format for all three components: position or job items, individuals and training experiences.

Assigning Levels of Competence for Knowledge and Skills

Again using the example of the physical resource management knowledge and skill areas, we will recall that we have already obtained importance weightings. Now what we need is a scale on which to measure levels of competence required for the position of physical resource manager (see Figure 4). Here we sacrifice ratio scale data in order to construct an assessment method which can be practically applied to each of our three components (position, person and training). We do this using an interval scale.

Let's assume we have averaged several interval ratings for "level of competence" required for the position and now possess average ratings for each knowledge and skill area (see Figure 5). Note that in this case the item, "travel proposal system," which carries the lowest weighted importance rating (refer back to Figure 2), is also rated lowest in terms of the level of competence required by the position (Figure 5). This close parallel between ratings is to be expected. However, note also that while the item labeled "supervisory activities" was rated as one of the three lowest in importance (Figure 2), it was relatively high on required level of competence for the position (Figure 5), achieving a 2.8. In other words, supervisory activities are normally not perceived as important to the successful performance of the job as many other areas of performance, but a fair level of competence is critical to successful job performance.

Figure 4
Rating Sheet—Levels of Competence
Required for Knowledge Areas and Skills of
Physical Resource Management

DIRECTIONS: Circle the most appropriate number to the right of each item.

Knowledge Areas

1. Facilities and construction management	1	2	3	4
2. Major capital repair and maintenance management procedures	1	2	3	4
3. Property and fund accountability systems	1	2	3	4
4. Travel proposal system	1	2	3	4

Skills

1. Problem definition	1	2	3	4
2. Priority setting	1	2	3	4
3. Program planning	1	2	3	'4
4. Program execution and coordination	1	2	3	4
5. Program review and evaluation	1	2	3	4
6. Interpersonal interactions	1	2	3	4
7. Supervisory activities	1	2	3	4

Descriptors

1 - Little or no knowledge/skill is required

2 - A moderate level of knowledge/skill is required

3 - A high level of knowledge/skill is required

4 - Expert knowledge/skill is required

Figure 5
Average Ratings for Knowledge and Skill
Levels of Competence for Physical Resource Management

Knowledge Areas	Competence Level Required
1. Facilities and construction management	2.4
2. Major capital repair and maintenance management procedures	3.5
3. Property and fund accountability systems	1.3
4. Travel proposal system	0.7
Skills	
1. Problem definition	2.1
2. Priority setting	3.2
3. Program planning	1.6
4. Program execution and coordination	3.7
5. Program review and evaluation	1.4
6. Interpersonal interactions	3.1
7. Supervisory activities	2.8

Assessing the Individual's Level of Competence

Next we turn to the rating of the individual on the major knowledge and skill items (see Figure 6). Note that we use the same interval scale format as when rating the level of competence required for the position. We noted earlier that this could be a self-appraisal or an appraisal by the individual's immediate supervisor, or a combination of both. Figure 7 shows a combined set of ratings for this same individual—his or her own and the supervisor's.

Figure 6
Rating Sheet—Levels of Competence on
Knowledge and Skill Areas for a Physical Resource Manager

Name: _____

DIRECTIONS: Circle the number on the right that best represents your level of competence (or your subordinate's if you are rating him or her).

Knowledge Areas

1. Facilities and construction management	1	2	3	4
2. Major capital repair and maintenance management procedures	1	2	3	4
3. Property and fund accountability systems	1	2	3	4
4. Travel proposal system	1	2	3	4

Skills

1. Problem definition	1	2	3	4
2. Priority setting	1	2	3	4
3. Program planning	1	2	3	4
4. Program execution and coordination	1	2	3	4
5. Program review and evaluation	1	2	3	4
6. Interpersonal interactions	1	2	3	4
7. Supervisory activities	1	2	3	4

Descriptors

1. I have (he or she has) little or no skill in this area.

2. I have (he or she has) a moderate level of skill in this area.

3. I have (he or she has) a high level of skill in this area.

4. I consider myself (him or her) an expert in this area.

Figure 7
Rating of Individual A on Knowledge and Skills Areas for Physical Resource Management

Knowledge Areas	*Individual's Rating
1. Facilities and construction management	2.0
2. Major capital repair and maintenance management procedures	1.0
3. Property and fund accountability systems	2.5
4. Travel proposal system	0.5
Skills	
1. Problem definition	3.0
2. Priority setting	3.0
3. Program planning	2.5
4. Program execution and coordination	2.5
5. Program review and evaluation	1.5
6. Interpersonal interactions	2.0
7. Supervisory activities	2.0

*Combination of individual's self-appraisal and the appraisal of the individual's immediate supervisor.

With this set of individual competence ratings, we are in a position to see whether the person in question has been assessed below the competence level required for the position (see Figure 8). In this case, the individual has been rated below the required competence level on seven items. The last column of Figure 8 shows the degree of deficiency and denotes it as "potential gain." That denotation reflects the realization that improvement in competence is of practical value as long as it approaches or meets the required level of competence for the position. For example, if a training course in supervision resulted in the individual becoming highly competent in "supervisory activities," he or she might thereafter rate himself or herself at 3 or 3.5 on that item. However, the potential gain for purposes of job performance would only be the difference between the former rating (2.0) and the required level of competence in that skill area for the position (2.8).

Figure 8
Competence Levels Compared with
Individual A's Ratings Yields Potential Gains Through Training

Knowledge Areas	Competence Level Required	A's Ratings	Potential Gains
1. Facilities and construction management	2.4	2.0	.4
2. Major capital repair and maintenance management procedures	3.5	1.0	2.5
3. Property and fund accountability systems	1.3	2.5	-
4. Travel proposal system	0.7	0.5	.2
Skills			
1. Problem definition	2.1	3.0	-
2. Priority setting	3.2	3.0	.2
3. Program planning	2.6	2.5	.1
4. Program execution and coordination	3.7	2.5	1.2
5. Program review and evaluation	1.4	1.5	-
6. Interpersonal interactions	3.1	2.0	1.1
7. Supervisory activities	2.8	2.0	.8

Determining Potential Gains Through Training

So far we have examined the position requirements and the individual's level of competence in relationship to those requirements. Now we turn to the training. Our intent is to determine to what degree a given training event will satisfy the need for increased competence in one or more of the identified knowledge or skill areas.

Earlier in this chapter we posed the question of how to attribute a value to a time management course for managers, and we implied that the skills of planning and prioritizing were central to the course. What is suggested here is that a training event does not have a fixed intrinsic value but rather a unique value for each potential participant, depending upon his or her job and his or her present level of competence in those areas the training addresses. For example, in Figure 8 we have composite ratings for Individual A. Note that for the skills of "priority setting" and "program planning," this individual already comes very close to the skill levels required for the position. Therefore, time management holds very little value for the individual *vis a vis* the position.

Look again at Figure 8 and note in the skill areas of "program execution and coordination" and "interpersonal interactions" that relatively large discrepancies exist between the required competence levels and the individual's ratings. The largest discrepancy lies in the knowledge areas of "major capital repair and maintenance procedures." These are the areas of competence that need the greatest attention (see the "potential gains" column in Figure 8).

At this point, we need to reconsider what it is we have once we arrive at a "potential gain" figure. It represents the difference between the stipulated competency level required for a given knowledge or skill area and the level attributed to the rated individual. More accurately, it represents the difference between aggregate ratings on matched interval scales, one set for the position, the other for the individual. Because we are dealing with (1) only one or a few raters; and (2) interval scales as opposed to ratio, we cannot assume that where we have, say, a potential gain of 1.0 that the potential value of the training is one-fourth of the individual's salary tied to that skill. That would be convenient but misleading. Rather, we need to establish a few conservative but reasonable rules for attributing potential value to the training.

Since we do not have scales that have been tested for validity or inter-rater reliability, we should require a relatively large deficiency factor to consider it sufficient evidence of need for performance improvement. We may arbitrarily set that factor at .5 or even 1.0. At the latter level (see Figure 9), we find only three of the knowledge/skill areas in which our hypothetical individual shows a deficiency large enough to signify potential performance improvement or gain through training.

Figure 9
Potential Gains for Individual A
Through Training and Related Dollar Values

Knowledge Areas	Portion of Average Annual Salary	Potential Gains	Potential Values of Training
1. Facilities and construction management	$3,096	.4	$ -
2. Major capital repair and maintenance management procedures	4,140	2.5	4,140
3. Property and fund accountability systems	1,620	-	-
4. Travel proposal system	1,260	.2	-
Skills			
1. Problem definition	1,836	-	-
2. Priority setting	4,248	.2	-
3. Program planning	5,004	-	-
4. Program execution and coordination	7,020	1.2	7,020
5. Program review and evaluation	2,124	-	-
6. Interpersonal interactions	3,960	1.1	3,960
7. Supervisory activities	2,700	.8	-

Notice in Figure 9 that for each of the three areas in which the discrepancy reaches or exceeds 1.0, the potential value of training is given as identical to the portion of the individual's salary attributed to the area (we obtained this from the weighting process depicted in Figure 3). Again, this is because the scale ratings do not allow us to infer how much a slight improvement in performance might be worth (or how large). Our decision to use the identical value attributed the "portion of salary" for a given item is based on a simple binary process. Either the individual and the supervisor believe that he or she can perform adequately in the given knowledge or skill area or they believe he or she cannot. If he or she can, then training theoretically will have no value for him or her in terms of job performance. If he or she cannot, then training is potentially worth the full value of the knowledge or skill for the position.

Weighing Training Value Against Training Cost

Thus our hypothetical physical resource manager presumably has much to gain from training which addresses:

1. The knowledge area of major capital repair and maintenance management procedures.
2. The skill area of program execution and coordination.
3. The skill area of interpersonal interactions.

Two things remain: (1) to ascertain that the proposed training is in fact designed to meet the needs projected for the individual; and (2) to compare the potential value of the training with its actual or projected cost.

In a way, we have come full circle from the beginning of the book, for here we are talking about the assessment of a particular training event, and we have considered in this text the steps of identifying learning objectives, analyzing the measurement instruments, reviewing instructional materials and observing instructional activities where feasible. However, unless an organization were going to send several people through the same expensive training program, it would not pay to have someone perform thorough evaluation of the training just to determine whether it was worth taking.

Rather, a critical examination of course objectives and/or descriptive material will have to suffice. At the same time, if the trainer or evaluator believes that several more persons may wish to take the course or program in question, he or she should at least thoroughly debrief the first learner as soon as possible after the training is completed.

Whatever means are used, the evaluator is looking for a match between learner needs and training intent or training results. If the individual wishes to take a course in probability theory because he or she has an identified need for improvement in organizational goal setting and program planning, the evaluator should at least determine whether the course as described will attempt to deal with its topic in a way that (1) reasonably relates to organizational goal setting and program planning; and (2) meets the level of skill or knowledge required in the individual's job or the job for which he or she is preparing.

So, for example, let's assume that goal setting and program planning were rated 3.0 for the individual's position (requiring a high level of knowledge or skill), and that the individual and the supervisor had rated him or her at 2.0 in that area (indicating that he or she possesses only a moderate level of knowledge or skill). In order for the course in probability theory to hold sufficient value for him or her, it would have to be aimed at achieving a fairly high level of skill development or knowledge acquisition. Thus the course must not only address the skill or knowledge in question, but also the level of competence the learner needs in the context of his or her work.

There is yet another wrinkle in this method of attributing value to a particular training experience. Probability theory may indeed strengthen an individual's competence, but it may represent only one small subset of skills and knowledge in the more comprehensive ability to set goals and plan programs. Therefore, we may have to compare one course with another in terms of not only what level of development they address, but how directly or comprehensively they deal with the individual's need. Thus, a course entitled *Goal Setting and Planning for the Manager* may be more appropriate to the person's need than *Probability Theory*.

Let's assume now that the portion of our individual's position attributed to goal setting and program planning is five percent and his or her salary is $40,000. That means this position item is valued at $2,000. Let's also assume that both the probability theory course and the goal setting/planning course are geared to a high level of skill development. One thing remains—to place estimated values on the two courses. We may reason that because the probability theory course will not result in improved goal setting and planning, we cannot attribute full value to it. We can only say that at best it will be worth something less than $2,000. We may also reason that the goal setting/planning course has the potential of being worth the full $2,000. In the absence of any further considerations, we would have had to judge the goal setting/planning course to be the better investment for the manager.

Designing an Individual Development Plan

Suppose we are developing with our hypothetical physical resource manager an individual development plan which is geared to offer him or her and his or her organization the strongest training options available at this time. We have at our disposal a list of courses from various vendors as well as the results from computing potential gains and potential values of training related to his or her professional development needs (refer back to Figure 9).

The list of courses includes the following:
- Basic Capital Repair and Maintenance Management
- Principles of Program Management
- Methods for Effective Interpersonal Communication

In reviewing our manager's profile (shown in Figure 8), we note the three items in which potential gain through training exceeds one full point on the interval scale. We match those position items with the courses, examining the courses for their levels of skill or knowledge development. We might derive something like the following comparison:

Item	Required Level	Course	Estimated Level
2 Major capital repair and maintenance	3.5	Basic Capital Repair and Maint. Management	2-2.5
4 Program execution and coordination	3.7	Principles of Program Management	3
6 Interpersonal interactions	3.1	Methods for Effective Interpersonal Communication	3-3.5

For capital repair we noted that the position requires a very high level of competence (3.5). Unfortunately, the course which matches in subject matter is meant only to convey basic knowledge. Therefore, our resource manager should opt for some other means for improving that performance area—perhaps another, more appropriate course or informal coaching from a more senior manager who has a reputation for excellent knowledge in the subject area.

For program execution and coordination, a very high level of competence is again required (3.7). Unfortunately, when we study the material on the course *Principles of Program Management*, we discover that it is geared to effect only a moderate level of skill development. Furthermore, it fails to deal with methods for tracking activities, a subskill area which has been judged as critical to the manager's ability to coordinate his or her program. Therefore, we may again recommend that other options be pursued for improving that skill area.

For interpersonal interactions, a fairly high level of competence is required (3.1). An analysis of material for the course, *Methods for Effective Interpersonal Communication,* reveals a course that is geared to effect high levels of performance in interpersonal interactions. It is a relatively expensive course at a total cost of $2,500 to the organization, but when we place that cost next to the potential value of training (shown in Figure 9), we see that the potential value ($3,960) easily offsets the cost of training in the first year following the training. Therefore, we can recommend this course as an investment both for the individual's professional and personal development and for the organization's benefit. Of course, we temper our expectations with the caveat that the course may not deliver what it promises. Obviously, if we can learn more about the course from someone who has recently attended it, we can make our recommendations with more certainty.

Conclusion

The point of this chapter is that both the costs and benefits of training can be calculated. Admittedly, the costs of training are easier to establish than the benefits. But the benefits can also be weighed and measured. The evaluator or trainer may tap the resources within the organization to identify costs which are associated with substandard performance and which may be reduced through training. He or she can employ job analysis to determine the relative importance of various skills and knowledge areas and can attribute salary or wage percentages to each. He or she can devise means for rating individuals on those skills and knowledge areas, and he or she can identify the potential any given training opportunity holds for the individual. In short, the evaluator or trainer can present management with a clear picture of what training will cost the organization and what it will gain for it in terms of developed human potential, reduced error and waste or increased productivity.

Review of Progress

Evaluator Task #6: Assess the costs and benefits associated with training.

Enabling Skills:
- Ability to calculate the costs of training.
- Ability to project the cost of alternatives to training.
- Ability to price the effects of substandard performance.
- Ability to project costs and benefits for non-technical training.
- Ability to project costs and benefits for individual development.

Chapter Note:
I am indebted to Garland Phillips, with whom I worked at the U.S. Office of Personnel Management. He led the effort in developing the kind of methodology I have described for projecting training values onto non-technical training programs.

Chapter 8

What Training Do We Need the Most?

In the previous chapter, we considered methods for calculating the costs of training. We also considered ways of estimating the benefits of training. Armed with those methods, the trainer or the evaluator is able to project for decision makers the relative advantages or disadvantages of supporting particular training events, whether workshops, courses or entire programs.

Methods for calculating cost-benefit relationships can greatly assist the trainer or training manager as he or she argues for supporting a new training effort or for maintaining an existing training effort in the face of organizational cutbacks. However, portraying the benefits of training in economic terms is still not enough in many instances. A training manager may be able to make a strong case for supporting a training budget of $500,000 in terms of projected return on investment, but if the organization simply cannot afford to spend $500,000 or chooses not to risk that level of investment, then another method of analysis is called for.

A Method for Prioritizing Training Programs

Essentially, what the trainer or evaluator must help the decision maker do is set priorities for spending or cost-reduction. If an organization can afford only to invest in one new training endeavor or to enhance one training program, which one will yield the greatest value? If an organization must sacrifice one training endeavor or must reduce the level of effort in several, where will it hurt the least? The following steps are offered as a way of answering those questions.

1. Compute and rank the cost of each training program. The means for computing training costs are described in Chapter 7. This is no small undertaking. What is suggested here is that in order to prioritize the relative cost-benefits of an organization's training efforts, each of those efforts must be accounted for in terms of what it costs the organization to develop, implement and maintain it.

Let's assume we analyze training costs for a large organization and come up with the profile shown in Figure 1. As you can see, the greatest single training investment made by this organization goes to support entry-level technical training. Not far behind it is "upward mobility," a euphemism for assisting employees to improve their career potential by pursuing undergraduate or graduate programs at local colleges and universities. Thus, these two training programs are ranked first and second according to cost.

2. Prioritize each training component according to its perceived potential value to the organization. This is a very subjective task. Therefore, it is best accomplished with the assistance of key people whose opinions count with the decision maker. Figure 2 displays one approach to gathering data on perceived potential value.

Figure 1

Training Program Costs

Training Component	Cost Per Year	Rank
1. Executive Development Program	$ 90,000	3
2. Upward Mobility Program	175,000	2
3. Secretarial training	50,000	'7
4. Equal opportunity training	35,000	8
5. Supervisory training	75,000	4
6. Communication skills training	10,000	11
7. Basic adult education	70,000	5
8. Technical training:		
• Entry-level	190,000	1
• To improve performance	60,000	6
• For program change	15,000	10
9. Orientation training	5,000	12
10. Management Intern Program	25,000	9

This approach forces the rater to make relative value judgments rather than simply state that some programs are absolutely essential to the organization and thus should not be questioned. Let's suppose we had asked six key people to rank the training programs in question. We would simply average the rankings for each component or program.

Our purpose in asking the raters to assess the components' potential rather than their actual value to the organization is to avoid having very important programs underrated simply because they are not implemented effectively. One presumably would want to improve a program with high potential value, not eliminate it. On the other hand, one may wish to eliminate a program with low potential value, even if it is effectively carried out.

Figure 2

Estimating the Potential Value
of Training—A Ranking Instrument

DIRECTIONS: Rank each of the training components below. Assume for this exercise that each training component is very effectively carried out, for we are estimating the "potential" value to the organization, as distinct from whatever actual impact the training may have.

1. If you could support only *one* of these effectively carried out training components, which one would it be? Place a (1) next to that component.
2. If you could support only *two* of these training components, which would be the *second* program you would choose?
3. Repeat this process until you have assigned successive rankings to each component.

Training Component	Rank (1-12)
1. Executive Development Program	____
2. Upward Mobility Program	____
3. Secretarial training	____
4. Equal opportunity training	____
5. Supervisory training	____
6. Communication skills training	____
7. Basic adult education	____
8. Technical training:	
• Entry-level	____
• To improve performance	____
• For program change	____
9. Orientation training	____
10. Management Intern Program	____

3. Judge the general effectiveness of training. Boldness is required in this step if it is to be done quickly, for one always runs the risk of being accused of doing too limited a study. However, the magnitude of the effort prohibits any kind of in-depth analysis of every training component. The thorough evaluation of a one-week course, using the Participant Action Plan Approach described in Chapter 5, can take as much as three weeks of intensive effort.

It is far more expedient to do quick, structured interviews of a small sample of trainees and their managers who are in a position to observe the effects of training on employee performance. A dozen interviews for each program (given 12) means 144 interviews. One-half hour a piece for interviewing, coding and extracting information for analysis means 72 hours, a task which can be accomplished within a two- to three-week period of work. It might appear even more expedient to conduct a mail survey, but much quality of data is lost in the form of unreturned surveys and forced-choice responses.

The interviewer may ask the following questions of the trainee:
a. Is it clear what you were supposed to have learned?
b. Have you used your training on your job? If so, how?
c. Could you have become proficient in a short time without the training?

d. Do you have tasks or responsibilities which should have been covered by training but were not?

e. Did you learn much that hasn't been used on the job? If so, what?

f. Do you see any (other) major problems with the training?

The interviewer may pose these questions to the supervisor:

a. Are your people coming adequately equipped with the knowledge, skills and attitudes addressed by the training?

b. Is training really required for these major job functions?

c. Would additional training make much difference in performance. If so, in what skill, knowledge or attitude areas?

d. Would less training make much difference in performance?

From the data, some reasonably clear picture should emerge. It remains for the evaluator to assess the data sets and label each component of training as (1) effective; (2) unclear in its effect; or (3) ineffective.

Figure 3 gives a full picture of the results from applying the first three steps to our hypothetical organization's training programs. Note, for example, that "entry-level" technical training as a generic type is at once the most expensive and the one perceived as having the highest potential value to the organization. Note also that the training is assessed tentatively as "effective." Thus, from this analysis we may conclude that the relatively high cost of entry level technical training is justified by virture of its perceived relative potential value and its perceived effectiveness.

On the other hand, the upward mobility program shows as one relatively high in cost but low in perceived value to the organization. Furthermore, the program has been judged as ineffective. This can be a politically sensitive program since it usually represents for minorities an alternate means of advancement in the organization. Management might wish to continue its support on philosophical or political grounds but at the same time investigate ways of making it more effective and/or less expensive. Or it may look for a more effective means for granting promotional opportunities to minorities.

Consider another component—orientation training. Its cost is minimal but apparently its potential for achieving good is also very limited. This is a prime target for elimination, albeit a small one. Just a word of caution, however. This action presumes that the evaluator has verified that the employees perceived the orientation as having relatively little potential value. If they feel otherwise, that perception would have to be weighed against the perception of the key people who rated the training components.

Suppose we found through an organizational analysis that one particular problem kept surfacing—e.g., the need for better supervisory performance in the areas of delegation of authority, communication with subordinates, setting work standards and evaluating work performance. Figure 3 shows us that the supervisory training program is relatively expensive and that it is perceived as having relatively high potential value for the organization. Yet the training has been rated as ineffective.

The evaluator can use this profiled data to support a recommendation that a more thorough evaluation be made of the supervisory training program for the purpose of defining how it may be made more effective in meeting its purposes. Such an evaluation would have its own costs, but the potential benefits in terms of more effective supervision should far outweigh the cost of evaluating and even redesigning the training.

Figure 3

Training Component Evaluation Worksheet

Training Component	Relative Cost	Relative Potential Value	Effectiveness of Training
1. Executive Development Program	2	3	Unclear
2. Upward Mobility Program	3	10	Ineffective
3. Secretarial training	7	8	Effective
4. Equal opportunity training	8	6	Unclear
5. Supervisory training	4	4	Ineffective
6. Communication skills training	11	9	Unclear
7. Basic adult education	5	11	Unclear
8. Technical training			
• Entry-level	1	1	Effective
• To impove performance	6	2	Effective
• For program change	10	7	Effective
9. Orientation training	12	12	Unclear
10. Management Intern Program	9	5	Unclear

5. Fixing the cost of evaluation. Once the trainer or evaluator has successfully instituted a reasonable cost-benefit approach to training decisions, he or she should be prepared to be asked what a given evaluation activity might cost and whether it is worth the effort. (To price an evaluation endeavor, one first has to determine just what methodology he or she will use and how much effort the method will require in this particular case. An example of pricing is shown in Appendix A.) Suppose an analysis had shown that rather than supervisory training, the most urgent need seems to be for assessment of the Upward Mobility Program and the Executive Development Program. The fact that they are both expensive and that in either case the effectiveness of training is in doubt suggests that these two programs certainly warrant evaluation.

Suppose we work up a preliminary outline of how we would go about evaluating each program and we estimate the cost of each evaluation (see Figure 4). Here we see that the cost to evaluate the Upward Mobility Program is projected at $25,000 (column 4) and that the program should last four years before it needs major alteration or reassessment. In other words, the evaluation should be good for four years. When we divide the cost of the evaluation ($25,000) by the annual cost of training ($175,000), then divide again by the number of years for which the evaluation should remain valid (4), we get 3.5 percent. In other words, for every $100 spent on the program *per se*, we project spending an additional $3.50 for evaluation.

Note in Figure 4 that when we do the same thing for the Executive Development Program, the results are much different. The program costs less, but the evaluation methodology projected would cost three times that of the methodology to be used for the Upward Mobility Program assessment. Furthermore, it is anticipated that this evaluation would be valid for only three years, not four. (There is no certain formula for estimating the "life" of an evaluation. Experience and common sense suggest that some training will need to change very rapidly to meet changes in technology and methodology. Where this is true, the evaluation will be good for the length of time the training can stand essentially as is and no longer. Conversely, the more stable the training, the longer the evaluation will be valid.)

Figure 4

Cost Comparison Sheet on Training and Training Evaluation

Training Component	Cost of Training	Method of Computation	Projected Cost of Evaluation	*Evaluation Cost as % of Cost of Training	Acceptable Cost?
Upward Mobility Program	$175,000 per year	Amortized over 4 years	$25,000	3.5%	YES
Executive Development Program	$ 90,000 per year	Amortized over 3 years	$ 75,000	28%	NO

*Actual Evaluation Cost	÷	No. Years Training Can Be	=	Evaluation Cost as
Annual Cost of Training		Used Without Reassessment		Percentage of Cost of Training

There is no absolute rule for determining how much or what percentage of a program's budget should be spent on evaluation. It depends upon how important the program is, how badly it needs evaluation and whether there are different methods which vary in cost but nevertheless render sufficient information to meet evaluation needs. And of course, most organizational budgets do have limits.

A decision maker might look at Figure 4 and decide that a thorough evaluation of the Upward Mobility Program is affordable, funding it at $25,000, but that such an assessment as that projected for the Executive Development Program is not affordable. The decision-maker might, however, ask for a less expensive alternative. In fact, whenever the evaluator can anticipate that the most effective means for assessing training will be denied because of its prohibitive cost, he or she should be prepared to present alternatives which preserve the essential integrity of the evaluation's purpose but which cost a good deal less.

Summary

In this chapter, we have considered ways to help decision makers arrive at informed decisions regarding the funding of training efforts. Realizing that an organization often fails to support training at the level its training manager may believe appropriate, the trainer or evaluator can at least show decision makers the relative value of the organization's training endeavors and where funds can be most appropriately used.

Review of Progress

Evaluator's Task #7: Prioritize organizational training efforts in terms of their relative value to the organization.

Enabling Skills:

- Ability to achieve organizational consensus on the relative value of major training efforts.
- Ability to conduct preliminary assessments of training effectiveness in brief time periods.
- Ability to form recommendations to decision makers regarding the funding and evaluation of training efforts.

Appendix A

Evaluation Cost Worksheet

Activities	Methods	Staff Time Estimates
1. Evaluate the executive seminar and managerial seminar (the core courses in the program):	Observe seminars—	48 hours
a. Assess congruence between seminar intent and needs analysis.	Interview personnel who developed the seminars regarding objectives and activities—	12 hours
b. Define immediate outcomes of seminar.	Analyze seminar material, activities and results—	32 hours
c. Assess quality of seminar design and implementation.		
d. Assess impact of seminar on job behavior and attitudes.	Using critical incident approach, conduct structured interviews with a sample of participants—	80 hours
e. Assess degree of support in job environment for seminar objectives and participant changes.	Analyze new behaviors and attitudes reported in interviews—	16 hours
	Write report of evaluation—	16 hours
f. Assess participant perceptions of seminar value, its strengths and limitations.		
2. Evaluate program as a whole:		
a. Draw on profile of managers attending all seminars.	Review individual development plans and seminar rosters—	4 hours
b. Assess congruence between needs analysis and the intent of the optional seminars.	Interview personnel who developed optional seminars—	24 hours
c. Define gaps and overlaps among optional seminars and between optional and core seminars.	Analyze and compare objectives and seminar content at program level—	16 hours
	Conduct structured interviews with sample of participants (expansion of similar activity above)—	24 hours
d. Assess degree to which program is perceived to meet individual needs.		

Estimated staff time	=	272 hours
Evaluator cost ($15/hr.)	=	4,080.00
Secretarial support	=	500.00
Materials	=	200.00
Total evaluation cost	=	4,780.00

Chapter 9

Is Our Training Proactive or Reactive?

"Doug Doer" has been training manager for a moderate-sized organization for several years. Doug contracts out for most training needs but calls upon a few in-house personnel to help him deliver some training. He generally tries to handle supervisory training himself and is acknowledged as a trainer with good platform skills.

Despite Doug's ability to get along and his general reputation as a competent instructor, top management is reluctant to support training, frequently cutting his budget below what he considers a minimum level of support. At the same time, mid-level managers often go to Doug with requests for training to improve worker performance. Doug happily obliges them by arranging for whatever they ask for, and he has no funding problems in these instances since the requesting managers use their own funds to support the training. Doug enjoys being responsive to managers' needs, but he can't understand the lack of support for training from the top.

What would a careful analysis of the situation show? Here is a plausible account:

We interview a sample of managers at each level of management, asking them about training in the organization:

1. Have they seen specific instances where training has made a difference in job performance?

2. Have they asked for training as a means of solving a performance problem?

3. Was the performance problem analyzed for causes or did the manager presume the problem was a lack of knowledge or skill on the part of the performers?

We also interview Doug Doer and ask him essentially the same questions. We ask Doug whether he recommends or insists on a problem analysis before designing or contracting out for training.

We discover that Doug has simply accepted the managers' descriptions of their problems as training problems. One typical case involved the training of file clerks. A manager of a large division complained to Doug that the file clerks in her division didn't know how to use the procedural system developed to control the flow of claims paperwork. Essentially, they were to log in and log out every file, and they were to indicate destination for files leaving their storage location. They were to keep files properly ordered by code, and they were to file returning cases as quickly as possible.

The filing system had deteriorated badly over the last year. Some claims folders were found in transit without being identified as to destination or time removed from files. Large numbers of folders were improperly filed and, on numerous occasions, claims processor personnel had complained that their requests for specific case folders were either ignored or their delivery excessively delayed. The filing system problem was affecting the larger claims processing system, and the problem was getting progressively worse.

The division manager then asked Doug to train the file clerks in the filing procedural system. She speculated that with heavy turnover in the last year there were several filing clerks on the job who had never really learned the system. Doug dutifully set about designing the training. He found the system embarrassingly easy to learn himself and was therefore able to develop a one-day workshop for file clerks within a few weeks. Doug delivered the workshop, using hands-on experience with simulated files. He systematically observed the file clerks as they performed the simulated activities and was pleased to note that they all seemed to have grasped the system.

Unfortunately, the filing problem did not go away. Even more unfortunately, Doug had assumed it would and did not follow up to assess the effects of his training. What we find upon closer analysis is that the filing problem was not a training problem in the first place—something Doug could have discovered through problem analysis at the beginning.

Through interviewing a sample of filing clerks and claims processing personnel, we construct a picture of what was occurring. First, a physical inspection of the claims holding area reveals that case folders are stacked high in corners with no visible labels. We learn that for several months filing clerks have had to stack files outside the cabinets because the cabinets are no longer sufficient to hold an ever expanding set of claims folders. This condition caused immediate problems. When a particular cabinet drawer reached saturation, an extension of that drawer was created in a corner of the filing room. With several drawers having reached saturation, stacks of folders literally hid the corners from view. Any attempt to maintain a logical map of these extensions broke down months ago. Now "what folders are where" lies in the collective memories of the several file clerks.

This deteriorating situation has been exacerbated by excessive absenteeism. A file clerk who may have "created" a new cabinet drawer extension in a corner one day may not be on the job the following day when a request comes in for a folder from that batch of folders placed in a corner. Another file clerk searches the drawer, then must begin looking in corners for the missing folder.

We ask—why the absenteeism? The inspection and interviews give us ready answers. The work space is not only cluttered unattractively with stacks of folders everywhere, but the ventilation is inadequate. It is stuffy and warm with a musty smell.

Has the filing supervisor notified management of these problems—the inadequate cabinet space and poor ventilation? Yes. New cabinets have been on order for six months. Nobody seems to be able to do anything about the ventilation.

We also discover through talking to the filing clerks and claims processing personnel that several claims personnel have begun, over the last several months, to come into the filing area to remove case files, something they are not supposed to do. Because they were frustrated by the untimely delays in receiving requested claims folders, they had decided to take matters into their own hands.

Although inefficient from an industrial engineering point of view, this practice might not have further contributed to the break-down in the filing system except that many of the claims processing personnel were neglecting to properly sign out the folders they took. Thus the people complaining the most were major contributors to the system's woes.

Our analysis has revealed the true nature of the problem. All the training in the world could not have alleviated it, for it was not a matter of skill development, knowledge or even attitude. The file clerks knew how to do their job. They simply were unable to overcome the physical inadequacies of their work environment. Indeed, this problem belonged squarely on the shoulders of management. Yet the manager of the division saw it as a training problem. Our unfortunate trainer became an unwitting accomplice, much to his own eventual disadvantage, for the manager in question later complained to his superiors that Doer's training had apparently not been adequate—her clerks still did not know how to file!

The Proactive Trainer

The role of the trainer as organizational analyst has begun to emerge over the past several years in the training community. The ideal projection of the trainer in this role is one in which he or she periodically interacts with managers to define and analyze performance problems. In organizations which have industrial psychologists or organizational development specialists, the trainer may need to go no further than helping the manager understand that the problem cannot be solved or can only partially be solved through training, and that he or she needs to turn to these other specialists for assistance. In organizations which do not have access to someone else trained to define and analyze performance problems, the trainer may have to offer that service. To simply tell a manager that his or her problem is not a training problem and that you can't help him or her is neither constructive for the organization or for the trainer's image. The trainer really has no alternative but to help the manager obtain the right kind of help or render the assistance him- or herself. (Two of the most influential books on this subject are Robert Mager's *Analyzing Performance Problems* and Tom Gilbert's *Human Competence, Engineering Worthy Performance*.)

The Evaluator's Perspective

An evaluator who is asked to assess training in terms of its broadest impact on the organization must be fully cognizant of both the potential and the limitations of training. He or she can provide a comprehensive assessment by formulating answers to the following questions:

1. Are the intents of training clearly specified?
2. Do training activities consistently meet the intents?
3. Is the learner tested or observed so that we know that he or she has mastered a set of skills or a body of knowledge?
4. Is the impact of training systematically assessed?
5. Are the costs and benefits of training identified and weighed?
6. Are training programs prioritized for decision makers in terms of relative value and need for evaluation?
7. Does training tend to address problems that can be directly solved through training?
8. Does the trainer provide direction in the identification and solution of problems which training cannot solve?

If the evaluator can answer these questions, he or she will have rendered an invaluable service to an organization. This book has been dedicated to that end.

Review of Progress

Evaluator Task #8: Identify training as proactive or reactive.

Enabling Skills:
- Ability to identify root causes of performance problems.
- Ability to classify causes of performance problems as amenable, not amenable or partially amenable to training solutions.
